Collins

D1173353

OK
RY **&**

Portuguese

HarperCollins*Publishers*

Food section by Edite Vieira Phillips

Other languages in the *Collins Phrase Book & Dictionary* series:

FRENCH

GERMAN

GREEK

ITALIAN

SPANISH

These titles are also published in a language pack containing
60-minute cassette and phrase book

HarperCollins Publishers
Westerhill Road, Bishopbriggs, Glasgow G64 2QT
www.collins.co.uk

First published 1999
Copyright © HarperCollins*Publishers*
Reprint 10 9 8 7 6 5 4
Printed in Italy by Amadeus SpA

ISBN 0 00-472075 X

INTRODUCTION

Your *Collins Phrase Book & Dictionary* is a handy, quick-reference guide that will help you make the most of your stay abroad. Its clear layout will save you valuable time when you need that crucial word or phrase.

There are three main sections in this book:

Practical topics arranged thematically with an opening section **KEY TALK** containing vital phrases that should stand you in good stead in most situations.

PHRASES

Short easy phrases that can be adapted for your situation

practical tips are highlighted in yellow boxes

SIGNS ARE IN GREEN BOXES

replies you might hear are highlighted in red boxes

FOOD SECTION

Phrases for ordering drinks and food
A region by region description of Portuguese food with a note on Portuguese wine and other popular drinks
Drinks
Menu reader

DICTIONARY

English-Portuguese   Portuguese-English signs highlighted

And finally, a short **GRAMMAR** section explaining how the language works.

So, just flick through the pages to find the information you need. Why not start with pronouncing Portuguese on page 6. From there on the going is easy with your *Collins Phrase Book & Dictionary*.

CONTENTS

PRONOUNCING PORTUGUESE

*In order to make the pronunciation as clear as possible, we've broken up the words into syllables using hyphens in the transcriptions. The syllable to be stressed is shown in **heavy type**. Like English, Portuguese has more sounds than letters to write them with, so the same letter doesn't always stand for the same sound. Rather than try to understand the system behind how they work, just rely on the phonetic transcription under every phrase. Here is a brief explanation of the transcription and sounds it represents.*

Portuguese	sounds like	transcription	example
g**a**to	a as in p**a**t	*a*	**ga**-too
uma	uh as in moth**er**	*uh*	**oo**-muh
esta	e as in p**e**t	*e*	**esh**-tuh
ir	ee as in p**ee**k	*ee*	eer
olá	o as in p**o**t	*o*	o-**la**
p**o**r	oo as in p**oo**l	*oo*	poor
ma**i**s	i as in p**i**ne	*aee*	maeesh
oito	oi as in p**oi**nt	*oy*	**oy**-too
c**o**mo	aw as in p**a**wn	*aw*	**kaw**-moo
p**au**	ou as in p**ou**nd	*aoo*	paoo

NASALISED VOWELS

*Sometimes vowels have a nasal twang, pronounced partly through the nose as in French 'non', 'matin', etc. Any vowel written with a tilde [~] over it in Portuguese is nasalised, e.g. não, manhã. In the transcriptions we have used 'ñ' to show that the preceding vowel is nasalised: ten (tayñ), muito (**mweeñ**-too), com (kawñ), um (ooñ), manhã (man-**yañ**), não (naooñ).*

OTHER LETTERS

Portuguese letter	transcription	sounds like	example
ç	**s**	's' in sit	almoço (al-**maw**-soo)
nh	**n-y**	'ni' in onion	vinho (**veen**-yoo)
lh	**l-y**	'lli' in million	filho (**feel**-yoo)
ch	**sh**	'sh' in shirt	chá (sha)
h	(always silent)		
j	**zh**	's' in pleasure	gelado (zhuh-**la**-doo)
s (after vowel or at end of word)	**sh**	'sh' in shirt	esta (**esh**-tuh)
rr, r (at start of word)	**rr**	rolled	rolo (**rraw**-loo)

Portuguese has two forms of address, formal and informal. You should use the informal **tu** only when you know someone well; otherwise use **o senhor** for gentlemen or **a senhora** for ladies.

yes
sim
seeñ

no
não
naooñ

that's fine
está bem
shta bayñ

please
por favor
poor fa-vawr

thank you
obrigado(a) *(fem.)*
o-bree-ga-doo/-duh

de nada
duh na-duh
don't mention it

hello
olá
o-la

goodbye
adeus
a-de-oosh

good night
boa noite
baw-uh noyt

good morning *(until lunch)*
bom dia
bawñ dee-uh

good afternoon/evening *(until dusk)*
boa tarde
baw-uh tard

excuse me!
por favor!
poor fa-vawr

sorry!
desculpe!
dush-koolp

pardon?
como?
kaw-moo

Here is an easy way to ask for something… just add **por favor**

a…
um… *('o' words)*
ooñ…

a coffee
um café
ooñ ka-fe

2 coffees
dois cafés
doysh ka-fesh

uma… *('a' words)*
oo-muh…

a beer
uma cerveja
oo-muh suhr-vay-zhuh

2 beers
duas cervejas
doo-ush suhr-vay-zhush

a coffee and two beers, please
um café e duas cervejas, por favor
ooñ ka-fe ee doo-ush suhr-vay-zhush poor fa-vawr

KEY TALK

I'd like...
queria...
kree-uh...

we'd like...
queríamos...
kreea-moosh...

I'd like an ice cream
queria um gelado
kree-uh ooñ zhuh-*la*-doo

we'd like to visit...
queríamos visitar...
kreea-moosh vee-zee-*tar*...

do you have...?
tem...?
tayñ...

do you have any milk?
tem leite?
tayñ layt

do you have stamps?
tem selos?
tayñ **se**-loosh

do you have a map?
tem um mapa?
tayñ ooñ **ma**-puh

do you have cheese?
tem queijo?
tayñ **kay**-zhoo

how much is it?
quanto custa?
kwañ-too *koosh*-tuh

how much does ... cost?
quanto custa o/a...?
kwañ-too *koosh*-tuh oo/uh...

how much is the cheese?
quanto custa o queijo?
kwañ-too **koosh**-tuh oo **kay**-zhoo

how much is the ticket?
quanto custa o bilhete?
kwañ-too **koosh**-tuh oo beel-**yet**

how much is a kilo?
quanto custa um quilo?
kwañ-too **koosh**-tuh ooñ **kee**-loo

how much is each one?
quanto é cada um?
kwañ-too e **ka**-duh ooñ

TOMATES..................... o KG		TOMATOES PER KILO
PERAS........................... o KG		PEARS PER KILO
LARANJAS .... cada		ORANGES EACH

where is...?
onde é...?
awñ-dee e...

where are...?
onde são...?
awñ-duh saooñ...

where is the station?
onde é a estação?
awñ-dee e uh shta-saooñ

where are the toilets?
onde são as casas de banho?
awñ-duh saooñ ush ka-sush duh ban-yoo

| **SENHORAS** LADIES | **LIVRE** FREE | **ENTRADA** ENTRANCE |
| **HOMENS** GENTS | **OCUPADO** ENGAGED | **SAÍDA** EXIT |

is there/are there...?
há...?
a...

is there a restaurant?
há um restaurante?
a ooñ rrush-to-rañt

where is there a chemist?
onde há uma farmácia?
awñ-dee a oo-muh far-mas-ya

are there children?
há crianças?
a kree-yañ-sush

is there a swimming pool?
há piscina?
a pshee-na

there is no...
não há...
naooñ a...

there is no hot water
não há água quente
naooñ a ag-wuh keñt

there are no towels
não há toalhas
naooñ a twal-yush

I need...
preciso de...
pruh-see-zoo duh...

I need a taxi
preciso de um táxi
pruh-see-zoo dooñ tak-see

I need to send a fax
preciso de mandar um fax
pruh-see-zoo duh mañ-dar ooñ faks

KEY TALK

can I...?
posso...?
po-soo...

can we...?
podemos...?
poo-de-moosh...

can I pay?
posso pagar?
po-soo pa-gar

can we go in?
podemos entrar?
poo-de-moosh eñ-trar

where can I...?
onde posso...?
awñ-duh po-soo...

where can I buy bread?
onde posso comprar pão?
awñ-duh po-soo kawñ-prar paooñ

where can I hire bikes?
onde posso alugar bicicletas?
*awñ-duh poss-oo a-loo-gar
bee-see-kle-tush*

pode comprar bilhetes no quiosque
pod kom-prar beel-yetsh noo kee-oshk
you can buy tickets at the kiosk

when?
quando?
kwañ-doo

at what time...?
a que horas...?
uh kee o-rush...

when is breakfast?
a que horas é o pequeno almoço?
uh kee o-rush e oo puh-ke-noo al-maw-soo

when is dinner?
a que horas é o jantar?
uh kee o-rush e oo zhañ-tar

when does it open?
quando abre?
kwañ-doo a-bruh

when does it close?
quando fecha?
kwañ-doo fay-shuh

yesterday
ontem
awñ-tayñ

today
hoje
awzh

tomorrow
amanhã
a-man-yañ

this morning
hoje de manhã
ozh duh man-yañ

this afternoon
hoje à tarde
awzh-a tard

tonight
hoje à noite
awzh-a noyt

10

ABERTO	OPEN
FECHADO	CLOSED
TODOS OS DIAS	DAILY
DIAS ÚTEIS	WEEKDAYS *(Mon-Sat)*
FERIADOS	HOLIDAY/SUNDAY

2ª	MON
3ª	TUE
4ª	WED
5ª	THU
6ª	FRI
SÁB.	SAT
DOM.	SUN

is it open?
está aberto
*shta a-**ber**-too*

is it closed?
está fechado?
*shta fuh-**sha**-doo*

2 HORAS	2 HOURS
3 HORAS	3 HOURS

abre às nove
a-brash nov
it opens at 9

o museu está fechado à segunda-feira
*oo moo-**ze**oo shta fuh-**sha**-doo a se-**gooñ**-duh **fay**-ruh*
the museum is closed on Mondays

GETTING TO KNOW PEOPLE

*The equivalent of Mr is **Senhor**, and Mrs, Ms and Miss is **Senhora**.*

how are you?
como está?
kaw-moo shta

fine, thanks. And you?
bem, obrigado(da). E você?
*bayñ o-bree-**ga**-do(-duh) ee vo-**se***

my name is...
chamo-me...
***sha**-moo-muh...*

what is your name?
como se chama?
***kaw**-moo suh **sha**-muh*

I don't understand
não compreendo
*naooñ kawñ-pree-**yeñ**-doo*

do you speak English?
fala inglês?
fa**-luh eeñ-**glesh

MONEY – changing

CASA DE CÂMBIO	BUREAU DE CHANGE
CAIXA AUTOMÁTICO	CASH DISPENSER

*Banks are generally open from 8.30am-3pm Mon-Fri. Bureaux de change (**casa de câmbio**) are not as common as banks and the exchange rates are less favourable. The easiest way of changing money is using your cashpoint card at a cash dispenser – look out for the **M** (**Multibanco**) sign.*

where can I change money?
onde se pode trocar dinheiro?
*awñ-duh suh pod troo-**kar** deen-**yay**-roo*

where is the bank?
onde é o banco?
*awñ-dee e oo **bañ**-koo*

where is the bureau de change?
onde é a casa de câmbio?
*awñ-dee e uh **ka**-suh duh **kañ**-bee-oo*

when does the bank open?
quando abre o banco?
*kwañ-doo **a**-bruh oo **bañ**-koo*

when does the bank close?
quando fecha o banco?
*kwañ-doo **fay**-shuh oo **bañ**-koo*

I want to cash these traveller's cheques
quero trocar estes cheques de viagem
***ke**-roo troo-**kar** **esh**-tush sheksh duh vee-**a**-zhayñ*

what is the rate...?
qual é o câmbio...?
*kwal e oo **kañ**-bee-oo...*

for pounds
da libra
*duh **lee**-bruh*

for dollars
do dólar
*doo **do**-lar*

I want to change £50
quero trocar cinquenta libras
***ke**-roo troo-**kar** seen-**kweñ**-tuh **lee**-brush*

where is there a cash dispenser?
onde há um caixa automático?
*awñ-dee a ooñ **kaee**-shuh aoo-too-**ma**-tee-koo*

I'd like small notes
queria notas pequenas
***kree**-uh **no**-tush puh-**ke**-nush*

spending – MONEY

CAIXA	CASH DESK	**IVA**	VAT

*Major credit cards are widely accepted in Portugal. Euros
(**eoo**-roosh) are used in Portugal. Euro cents are known as
cêntimos (sayñ-tee-**moosh**).*

how much is it?
quanto custa?
kwañ-too koosh-tuh

how much will it be?
quanto vai custar?
kwañ-too vaee kush-tar

I want to pay
queria pagar
kree-uh pa-gar

we want to pay separately
queremos pagar separadamente
kre-moosh pa-gar suh-pa-ra-da-meñt

can I pay by credit card?
posso pagar com o cartão de crédito?
po-soo pa-gar kawñ oo kar-taooñ duh kre-dee-too

do you accept traveller's cheques?
aceita traveller cheques?
a-say-tuh tra-ve-ler sheks

how much is it...?	**per person**	**per night**	**per kilo**
quanto é...?	por pessoa	por noite	por quilo
kwañ-too e...	*poor psaw-uh*	*poor noyt*	*poor kee-loo*

are service and VAT included?
está incluído serviço e IVA?
shta eeñ-kloo-ee-doo suhr-vee-soo ee ee-vuh

can I have a receipt, please?
queria um recibo por favor
kree-uh ooñ rruh-see-boo poor fa-vawr

do I pay a deposit?
deixo depósito?
day-shoo duh-po-zee-too

I've nothing smaller
não tenho troco
naooñ tayn-yoo traw-koo

keep the change
guarde o troco
gward oo traw-koo

13

AIRPORT

CHEGADAS	ARRIVALS
PARTIDAS	DEPARTURES
RECOLHA DE BAGAGEM	BAGGAGE RECLAIM
VOO	FLIGHT
ATRASO	DELAY

to the airport, please
ao aeroporto, por favor
*aoo e-ro-**pawr**-too poor fa-**vawr***

how do I get into town?
como se vai para o centro?
*kaw-moo suh vaee pa-ruh oo **señ**-troo*

where do I get the bus to the town centre?
onde apanho um autocarro para o centro?
***awñ**-duh-**pan**-yoo ooñ o-to-**ka**-rroo **pa**-ruh o **señ**-troo*

how much is it...?
quanto é...?
***kwañ**-too e...*

to the town centre
para o centro
***pa**-ruh oo **señ**-troo*

to the airport
ao aeroporto
*aoo e-ro-**pawr**-too*

where do I check in for...?
onde faço o check-in de...?
***awñ**-duh **fa**-soo oo chek-**een** duh...*

which gate is it for the flight to...?
qual é a porta de embarque do voo para...?
*kwal e uh **por**-tuh deñ-**bark** doo **vaw**-oo pa-ruh...*

o embarque será na porta número...
*oo eñ-**bark** suh-**ra** na **por**-ta **noo**-muh-roo...*
boarding will take place at gate number...

última chamada para os passageiros do voo...
***ool**-tee-muh sha-**ma**-duh **pa**-ruh pa-sa-**zhay**-roosh doo **vaw**-oo...*
last call for passengers on flight...

o seu voo está atrasado
*oo seoo **vaw**-oo shta a-tra-**za**-doo*
your flight is delayed

CUSTOMS & PASSPORTS

ALFÂNDEGA	CUSTOMS
CONTROLE DE PASSAPORTES	PASSPORT CONTROL
CIDADÃOS UE	EU CITIZENS

With the single European market, EU (European Union) citizens are subject to only highly selective spot checks and they can go through the blue customs channel (unless they have goods to declare). There is no restriction by quantity or value, on goods purchased by travellers in another EU country provided they are for their own personal use (guidelines have been published). If unsure, check with customs officials.

I have nothing to declare
não tenho nada a declarar
*naooñ **tayn**-yoo **na**-duh uh duh-kla-**rar***

here is...	**my passport**	**my green card**
aqui está...	o meu passaporte	o meu cartão verde
*a-**kee** shta...*	*oo meoo pa-sa-**port***	*oo meoo kar-**taooñ** verd*

do I have to pay duty on this?
é preciso pagar direitos para isto?
*e pruh-**see**-zoo pa-**gar** dee-**ray**-toosh pruh **eesh**-too*

it's for my own personal use
é para meu uso pessoal
*e **pa**-ruh meoo **oo**-zoo puh-**swal***

we're going to...
vamos a...
***va**-moosh uh...*

the children are on this passport
as crianças estão neste passaporte
*ush kree-**yañ**-sush shtaooñ nesht pa-sa-**port***

I'm...	**English** *(m/f)*	**Australian** *(m/f)*
sou...	inglês/inglesa	australiano(na)
saw...	*eeñ-**glesh**/een-**gle**-za*	*aoosh-tra-lee-**a**-noo(-nuh)*

15

ASKING THE WAY – questions

excuse me!
por favor!
*poor fa-**vawr***

where is...?
onde é...?
***awñ**-dee e...*

where is the nearest...?
onde é o/a ... mais próximo(ma)?
***awñ**-dee e oo/uh ... maeesh **pro**-see-moo(-muh)*

how do I get to...?
como se vai para...?
***kaw**-moo suh vaee **pa**-ruh...*

is this the right way to...?
a/o ... é por aqui?
*oo/uh... e poor a-**kee***

is this the right way to the museum?
o museu é por aqui?
*oo moo-**ze**oo e poor a-**kee***

the...   is it far?
a/o...   é longe?
oo/uh...   e lawñzh

is it far to...?
falta muito para...?
***fal**-tuh **mweeñ**-too **pa**-ruh...*

can I walk there?
posso ir a pé?
***po**-soo eer uh pe*

is there a bus that goes there?
há um autocarro para lá?
*a ooñ o-to-**ka**-rroo **pa**-ruh la*

we're looking for...
estamos à procura de...
***shta**-moosh a pro-**koo**-ruh duh...*

we're lost
estamos perdidos
***shta**-moosh puhr-**dee**-doosh*

can you show me on the map?
pode-me indicar no mapa?
***pod**-muh eeñ-dee-**kar** noo **ma**-puh*

answers – ASKING THE WAY

It's no use being able to ask the way if you're not going to understand the directions you get. We've tried to anticipate the likely answers, so listen carefully for these key phrases.

siga sempre em frente
see-guh señpr ayñ freñt
keep going straight ahead

tem que dar a volta
*tayñ kuh dar uh **vol**-tuh*
you have to turn round

vire ...
veer...
turn...

à direita
*a dee-**ray**-tuh*
right

à esquerda
*a **shker**-duh*
left

vá ...
va...
go...

sempre em frente
señpr ayñ freñt
straight on

siga sempre em frente
see-guh señpr ayñ freñt
keep going straight on

até chegar a...
*uh-**te** shuh-**gar** uh*
as far as...

tome...
tom...
take...

a primeira à direita
*uh pree-**may**-ruh a dee-**ray**-tuh*
the first on the right

a segunda à esquerda
*a suh-**gooñ**-duh a **shker**-duh*
the second on the left

a estrada para...
*a **shtra**-duh **pa**-ruh...*
the road to...

siga os sinais para...
*see-guh oosh see-**naeesh** pa-ruh...*
follow the signs for...

BUS

PARAGEM DE AUTOCARRO   BUS STOP

*Tickets and information on long-distance coach travel are available from travel agents and main bus stations. On local bus journeys you pay on the bus or buy 10 tickets at a time (**uma caderneta de módulos**) from newspaper kiosks.*

where is the bus station?
onde é a estação de autocarros?
*awñ-dee e uh stha-**saooñ** do-to-**ka**-rroosh*

I want to go...
quero ir para...
***ke**-roo eer **pa**-ruh...*

to the station
a estação
*a shta-**saooñ***

to the museum
ao museo
*aoo moo-**zeoo***

to the Gulbenkian
à Gulbenkian
a gulbenkian

to Rossio
ao Rossio
*aoo rroo-**seeoo***

is there a bus that goes there?
há um autocarro para lá?
*a ooñ o-to-**ka**-rroo **pa**-ruh la*

which bus do I take to go to...?
que autocarro apanho para...?
*kuh o-to-**ka**-rroo a-**pan**-yoo **pa**-ruh...*

where do I get the bus to...?
onde apanho um autocarro para...?
*awñ-da-**pan**-yoo ooñ o-to-**ka**-rroo **pa**-ruh...*

how often are the buses?
que frequência têm os autocarros?
*kuh fruh-**kweñ**-see-uh **tayñ**-ayñ oosh o-to-**ka**-rroosh*

when is the last bus?
a que horas é o último autocarro?
*a kee **o**-rush e oo **ool**-tee-moo o-to-**ka**-rroo*

can you tell me when to get off?
pode-me dizer quando devo sair?
***pod**-muh dee-**zer** **kwañ**-doo **de**-voo saer*

UNDERGROUND

METRO	UNDERGROUND
ENTRADA	ENTRANCE
SAÍDA	EXIT

*Buy your tickets at the underground station. You can also buy a 10-trip ticket (**uma caderneta de 10 viagens**) which is cheaper than individual tickets and can be used by different people.*

where is the metro station?
onde é a estação de metro?
*awñ-dee e uh shta-**saooñ** duh me-troo*

are there any special tourist tickets?
tem um bilhete especial para turistas?
*tayñ ooñ beel-**yet** shpuh-**seeal** pa-ruh too-**reesh**-tush*

do you have an underground map?
tem um mapa do metro?
*tayñ ooñ **ma**-puh doo me-troo*

I want to go to...
quero ir para...
***ke**-roo eer **pa**-ruh...*

can I go by underground?
posso apanhar o metro?
*po-soo a-pan-**yar** oo **me**-troo*

do I have to change?
tenho que mudar?
tayn**-yoo kuh moo-**dar

where?
onde?
***awñ**-duh*

which line is it for...?
qual é a linha para...?
*kwal e uh **leen**-yuh **pa**-ruh...*

what is the next stop?
qual é a próxima paragem?
*kwal e uh **pro**-see-muh puh-**ra**-zhayñ*

which is the station for the Gulbenkian?
qual é a estação para a Gulbenkian?
*kwal e uh shta-**saooñ pa**-ruh uh gulbenkian*

TRAIN

ALFA	INTERCITY EXPRESS
INTERCIDADES	INTERCITY
BILHETEIRA	TICKETS
INFORMAÇÕES	INFORMATION
PARTIDAS	DEPARTURES
CHEGADAS	ARRIVALS
PLATAFORMA	PLATFORM
VAGÃO RESTAURANTE	RESTAURANT CAR

*Ticket for the fast **Alfa** and **Intercidades** services can be booked at stations and travel agents up to 20 days in advance. You must have your ticket before boarding the train. Allow plenty of time if buying your ticket at the time of travel since queuing is likely. You can also purchase these tickets from **Multibanco** cash dispensers.*

where is the station?
onde é a estação?
*awñ-dee e uh shta-**saooñ***

to the station, please
à estação por favor
*a shta-**saooñ** poor fa-**vawr***

a single to...
um para...
*ooñ **pa**-ruh...*

2 singles to...
dois para...
*doysh **pa**-ruh...*

a return to...
um ida e volta para...
*ooñ **ee**-duh ee **vol**-tuh **pa**-ruh...*

2 returns to...
dois ida e volta para...
***do**-eesh **ee**-duh ee **vol**-tuh **pa**-ruh...*

a child's return to...
meio bilhete, ida e volta para...
***may**-oo beel-**yet ee**-duh ee **vol**-tuh **pa**-ruh...*

lst/2nd class
primeira/segunda classe
*pree-**may**-ruh suh-**gooñ**-duh klas*

smoking
fumador
*foo-ma-**dawr***

non smoking
não fumador
*naooñ foo-ma-**dawr***

do I have to pay a supplement?
paga-se suplemento?
pa-ga-suh soo-pluh-meñ-too

is my pass valid on this train?
este passe é valido neste comboio?
esht pas e va-lee-doo nesht kawñ-bo-yoo

I want to book...	**a seat**	**a couchette**
queria reservar...	um lugar	uma couchette
kree-uh rruh-suhr-var...	*ooñ loo-gar*	*oo-muh koo-shet*

can I have a timetable?
podia dar-me um horário?
poo-dee-uh dar-muh ooñ o-ra-reeoo

do I need to change?   **where?**
tenho que mudar?   onde?
tayn-yoo kuh moo-dar   *awñ-duh*

which platform does it leave from?
de que plataforma parte?
duh kuh pla-ta-for-muh part

does the train to ... leave from this platform?
é esta a plataforma do comboio para...?
e esh-tuh a pla-ta-for-muh doo kawñ-bo-yoo pa-ruh...

is this the train for...?
é este o comboio para...?
e esht oo kawñ-bo-yoo pa-ruh...

where is the left-luggage?
onde é o depósito de bagagens?
awñ-dee e oo duh-po-zee-too duh ba-ga-zhayñsh

is this seat free?
está livre?
shta leev-ruh

TAXI

You can either hail a taxi or call a taxi firm. A surcharge will apply if luggage is placed in the boot. A higher rate will be charged during the night and on weekends and public holidays. Two green lights on the roof of the car mean that the higher rate applies.

to the airport, please
ao aeroporto, por favor
*aoo e-ro-**pawr**-too poor fa-**vawr***

to the station, please
à estação, por favor
*a shta-**saooñ** poor fa-**vawr***

take me to this address, please
leve-me a esta morada, por favor
lev**-muh uh **esh**-tuh moo-**ra**-duh poor fa-**vawr

how much will it cost?
quanto vai custar?
kwañ**-too vaee koosh-**tar

how much is it to the centre?
quanto custa ao centro?
***kwañ**-too **koosh**-tuh aoo **señ**-troo*

it's too much
é caro demais
*e **ka**-roo duh-**maeesh***

where can I get a taxi?
onde se pode arranjar um táxi?
***awñ**-duh suh pod a-rrañ-**zhar** ooñ **tak**-see*

please order me a taxi
chame-me um táxi por favor
sha**-muh-muh ooñ **tak**-see poor fa-**vawr

can I have a receipt?
pode-me dar um recibo?
***pod**-muh dar ooñ rruh-**see**-boo*

I've nothing smaller
não tenho troco
*naooñ **tayn**-yoo **traw**-koo*

keep the change
guarde o troco
*gward oo **traw**-koo*

Tourist offices can give information on ferry services and boat trips in the resorts.

1 ticket
um bilhete
ooñ beel-yet

2 tickets
dois bilhetes
doysh beel-yetsh

single
de ida
dee-duh

round trip
de ida e volta
dee-duh ee vol-tuh

is there a tourist ticket?
há bilhete para turistas?
a beel-yet pa-ruh too-reesh-tush

are there any boat trips?
há excursões de barco?
a shkoor-soyñsh duh bar-koo

how long is the trip?
quanto dura a viagem?
kwañ-too doo-ruh a veea-zhayñ

when is the next boat?
quando parte o próxima barco?
kwañ-doo part oo pro-see-moo bar-koo

when is the next ferry?
quando parte o próximo ferry-boat?
kwañ-doo part oo pro-see-moo ferry-boat

when is the first boat?
a que horas é o primeiro barco?
a kee o-rush e o pree-may-roo bar-koo

when does the boat leave?
quando parte o barco?
kwañ-doo part oo bar-koo

do you have a timetable?
tem um horário?
tayñ ooñ o-ra-reeoo

when is the last boat?
a que horas é o último barco?
a kee o-rush e oo ool-tee-moo bar-koo

is there a restaurant on board?
o barco tem restaurante?
oo bar-koo tayñ rrush-to-rañt

can we hire a boat?
podemos alugar um barco?
po-de-moosh a-loo-gar ooñ bar-koo

CAR – driving/parking

TODAS AS DIRECÇÕES	ALL ROUTES
SAÍDA	EXIT
AUTO-ESTRADA	MOTORWAY
PORTAGEM	TOLL
ESTACIONAMENTO PROIBIDO	NO PARKING
CENTRO DA CIDADE	CITY CENTRE

To drive in Portugal visitors must have a valid pink EU driver's licence or an international licence and must be at least 18 years old. Drivers must at all times carry their licence, passport, the logbook or rental agreement and an insurance certificate. If you have an accident, contact the police immediately who will file a report. Tolls are payable on motorways and Lisbon bridges. Do not use the lane marked Via Verde.

can I park here?
pode-se estacionar aqui?
pod-suh shtas-yoo-nar a-kee

where can I park?
onde posso estacionar?
awñ-duh po-soo shtas-yoo-nar

is there a car park?
há um parque de estacionamento?
a ooñ park duh shtas-yoo-na-meñ-too

do I need a parking disc?
é preciso uma licença de estacionamento?
e pruh-see-zoo oo-muh lee-señ-suh duh shtas-yoo-na-meñ-too

where can I get a parking disc?
onde posso comprar uma licença de estacionamento?
awñ-duh po-soo kawñ-prar oo-muh lee-señ-suh duh shtas-yoo-na-meñ-too

how long can I park here?
quanto tempo posso estacionar aqui?
kwañ-too teñ-poo po-soo shtas-yoo-nar a-kee

we're going to...
vamos a...
va-moosh uh...

what's the best route?
qual é o melhor caminho?
kwa-le oo mel-yor ka-meen-yoo

SUPER	4 STAR
SEM CHUMBO	UNLEADED
GASÓLEO	DIESEL
GASOLINA	PETROL
BOMBA DE GASOLINA	PETROL PUMP

Green pumps are for unleaded petrol, blue ones for leaded and yellow ones for diesel.

is there a petrol station near here?
há uma garagem aqui perto?
*a **oo**-muh ga-**ra**-zhayñ a-**kee** per-too*

fill it up, please
encha, por favor
eñ**-shuh poor fa-**vawr

... euros worth of 4 star
... euros de super
*... **eoo**-roosh duh **soo**-per*

pump number...
bomba número...
***bawñ**-buh **noo**-muh-roo...*

that is my car
esse é o meu carro
*es e oo meoo **ka**-rroo*

where is the air line?
onde está o ar?
***awñ**-duh shta oo ar*

where is the water?
onde está a água?
***awñ**-duh shta a **ag**-wuh*

please check...
pode verificar...
*pod vuh-ree-fee-**kar**...*

the tyre pressure
a pressão dos pneus
*a pruh-**saooñ** doosh pneoosh*

the oil
o óleo
*oo **o**-lee-oo*

the water
a água
*uh **ag**-wuh*

que bomba?
*kuh **bawñ**-buh*
which pump?

CAR – problems/breakdown

When breaking down on a major road, use one of the orange SOS telephones. State whether you are entitled to breakdown cover.

I've broken down
o meu carro está avariado
oo meoo ka-rroo shta a-va-ree-a-doo

what do I do?
o que devo fazer?
o kuh de-voo fa-zer

I'm on my own *(female)*
estou sozinha
shto so-zeen-yuh

there are children in the car
há crianças no carro
a kree-yañ-sush noo ka-rroo

where's the nearest garage?
onde há uma oficina aqui perto?
awñ-dee a oo-muh o-fee-see-nuh a-kee per-too

is it serious?
é grave?
e grav

can you repair it?
pode arranjá-lo?
pod a-rrañ-zha-loo

how much will it cost?
quanto vai custar?
kwañ-too vaee kush-tar

when will it be ready?
quando estará pronto?
kwañ-doo shta-ra prawñ-too

the car won't start
o carro não pega
oo ka-rroo naooñ pe-guh

the engine is overheating
o motor está a aquecer demais
oo moo-tawr shta a a-ke-ser duh-maeesh

the battery is flat
a bateria está descarregada
uh ba-tuh-ree-uh shta dush-ka-rruh-ga-duh

have you the parts?
tem as peças?
tayñ ush pe-sush

it's not working
não anda
naooñ añ-duh

I have a flat tyre
tenho um furo
tayn-yoo ooñ foo-roo

can you replace the windscreen?
pode substituir o pára-brisas?
pod sub-shtee-tweer oo pa-ra-bree-zush

ALUGUER DE AUTOMÓVEIS CAR HIRE

Cars can be hired at airports and in towns and resorts. Drivers must be over 23 and hold a valid EU or international driver's licence.

I want to hire a car
queria alugar um carro
kree-uh a-loo-gar ooñ ka-rroo

for one day
para um dia
pa-ruh ooñ dee-yuh

for ... days
para ... dias
pa-ruh ... dee-ush

I want...
quero...
ke-roo...

a large car
um carro grande
ooñ ka-rroo grañd

a small car
um carro pequeno
ooñ ka-rroo puh-ke-noo

an automatic
um carro automático
ooñ ka-rroo aoo-too-ma-tee-koo

how much is it?
quanto é?
kwañ-too e

is fully comprehensive insurance included in the price?
inclui o seguro contra todos os riscos?
eeñ-kloo-ee oo suh-goo-roo kawñ-truh to-doosh oosh rreesh-koosh

what do we do if we break down?
o que devo fazer se o carro avariar?
o kuh de-voo fa-zer soo ka-rroo a-va-ree-ar

when must I return the car by?
a que horas tenho de devolver o carro?
uh kee o-rush tayn-yoo kuh duh-vol-ver oo ka-rroo

please show me the controls
podia mostrar-me os comandos?
po-dee-uh moosh-trar-muh oosh koo-mañ-doosh

where are the documents?
onde estão os documentos?
awñ-duh shtaooñ oosh do-koo-meñ-toosh

CAIXA	CASH DESK
SALDO	SALE

...m-7pm. In smaller towns and villages there is
...k varying from between 1-3pm. Big shopping
centres o... ...skirts of major towns open from 10am-11pm
seven days a week.

do you sell...?
vende...?
veñ-duh...

batteries for this camera
pilhas para esta máquina
peel-yush pa-ruh esh-tuh ma-kee-nuh

stamps
selos
se-loosh

where can I buy...?
onde posso comprar...?
awñ-duh po-soo kawñ-prar...

stamps
selos
se-loosh

films
rolos
rraw-loosh

10 stamps
dez selos
desh se-loosh

for postcards
para postais
pa-ruh poosh-taeesh

to Britain
para a Grã-Bretanha
pa-ruh uh grañ-bruh-tan-yuh

a colour film
um rolo a cores
ooñ rraw-loo uh kaw-rush

a tape for this video camera
uma cassette para esta câmara de vídeo
*oo-muh ka-set pa-ruh esh-tuh ka-ma-ruh duh
vee-deeoo*

I'm looking for a present
estou à procura de um presente
shtaw a pro-koo-ruh dooñ pruh-señt

have you anything cheaper?
não tem nada mais barato?
naooñ tayñ na-duh maeesh ba-ra-too

it's a gift
é para oferta
e pa-ruh o-fer-tuh

please wrap it up
podia embrulhá-lo?
poo-dee-uh eñ-brool-ya-loo

is there a market?
há algum mercado?
a al-gooñ muhr-ka-doo

when?
quando?
kwañ-doo

clothes – SHOPPING

WOMEN		MEN		SHOES			
UK	EU	UK	EU	UK	EU	UK	EU
8	36	36	46	2	35	7	40
10	38	38	48	3	36	8	42
12	40	40	50	4	37	9	43
14	42	42	52	5	38	10	44
16	44	44	54	6	39	11	45
18	46	46	56	7	41	12	46

can I try this on?
posso experimentar?
po-soo shpuh-ree-meñ-**tar**

it's too big
fica-me grande
fee-ka-muh grañd

it's too small
fica-me pequeno
fee-ka-muh puh-**ke**-noo

it's too expensive
é caro demais
*e ka-roo duh-**maeesh***

I'm just looking
estou só a ver
shtaw so a ver

I take a size ... shoe
calço o número…
kal-soo oo **noo**-muh-roo…

where are the changing rooms?
onde é o gabinete de provas?
***awñ**-dee e oo ga-bee-**net** duh **pro**-vush*

have you a smaller size?
tem uma medida mais pequena?
*tayñ **oo**-muh muh-**dee**-duh maeesh
puh-**ke**-nuh*

have you a larger size?
tem uma medida maior?
*tayñ **oo**-muh muh-**dee**-duh maee-**or***

I'll take this one
levo este
***le**-voo esht*

---

que número calça?
*kuh **noo**-muh-roo **kal**-suh*
what shoe size are you?

serve-lhe?
***ser**-vuhl-yuh*
does it fit?

SHOPPING – food

PADARIA BAKER'S	**SUPER-MERCADO** SUPERMARKET
TALHO BUTCHER'S	**FRUTARIA** GREENGROCER'S

You can buy fresh fruit, vegetables and other local produce from the market (o mercado). They are usually open in the mornings. In tourist resorts they may stay open until late afternoon.

where can I buy...?	**fruit**	**bread**	**milk**
onde posso comprar...?	fruta	pão	leite
*awñ-duh **po**-soo kawñ-**prar**...*	***froo**-tuh*	*paooñ*	*layt*

where is...?	**the supermarket**	**the baker's**
onde é...	o supermercado	a padaria
awñ-dee e...	*oo soo-per-muhr-**ka**-doo*	*uh pa-da-**ree**-uh*

where is the market?	**which day is the market?**
onde é o mercado?	que dia é o mercado?
*awñ-dee e oo muhr-**ka**-doo*	*kuh **dee**-uh e oo muhr-**ka**-doo*

it's my turn next	**that's enough**
sou eu a seguir	chega
*saw eoo a suh-**geer***	***she**-guh*

a litre of...	**milk**	**water**	**beer**
um litro de...	leite	água	cerveja
*ooñ **lee**-troo duh...*	*layt*	***ag**-wuh*	*suhr-**vay**-zhuh*

a bottle of...	**water**	**wine**	**olive oil**
uma garrafa de...	água	vinho	azeite
*oo-muh ga-**rra**-fuh duh...*	***ag**-wuh*	***veen**-yoo*	*a-**zayt***

a can of...	**coke**	**beer**	**tonic water**
uma lata de...	coca-cola	cerveja	água tónica
*oo-muh **la**-tuh duh...*	*ko-ka-**ko**-luh*	*suhr-**vay**-zhuh*	*ag-wuh **to**-nee-kuh*

a carton of...	**orange juice**	**milk**
um pacote de...	sumo de laranja	leite
*ooñ pa-**kot** duh...*	***soo**-moo duh luh-**rañ**-zhuh*	*layt*

food – SHOPPING

100 grams of...
cem gramas de...
*sayñ **gra**-mush duh...*

half a kilo of...
meio quilo de...
***may**-oo **kee**-loo duh...*

a kilo of...
um quilo de...
ooñ kee-loo duh...

8 slices of...
oito fatias de...
***oy**-too fa-**tee**-ush duh...*

a loaf of bread
um pão
ooñ paooñ

half a dozen eggs
meia dúzia de ovos
***may**-uh **doo**-zee-uh **do**-voosh*

a packet of...
um pacote de...
*ooñ pa-**kot** duh...*

a tin of...
uma lata de...
*oo-muh **la**-tuh duh...*

a jar of...
um frasco de
*ooñ **frash**-koo duh...*

cheese
queijo
***kay**-zhoo*

sausages
salsichas
*sal-**see**-shush*

potatoes
batatas
*ba-**ta**-tush*

cooked ham
fiambre
*fee-**añ**-bruh*

three yogurts
três iogurtes
*tresh yo-**goor**-tush*

biscuits
bolachas
boo-la-shush

tomatoes
tomates
*too-**ma**-tush*

jam
doce
daws

olives
azeitonas
*a-zay-**taw**-nush*

mushrooms
cogumelos
*kaw-goo-**me**-loosh*

apples
maçãs
*ma-**sañsh***

cured ham
presunto
*pruh-**zooñ**-too*

sugar
açúcar
*a-**soo**-kar*

peas
ervilhas
*er-**veel**-yush*

olives
azeitonas
*a-zay-**taw**-nush*

que deseja?
*kuh duh-**zay**-zhuh*
what would you like?

mais alguma coisa?
*maeesh al-**goo**-muh **koy**-zuh*
anything else?

SIGHTSEEING

TURISMO   TOURIST OFFICE

Tourist offices will provide town plans, information on accommo-
dation, restaurants and local attractions.

where is the tourist office?
onde é o centro de turismo?
*awñ-dee e oo **señ**-troo duh too-**reezh**-moo*

we'd like to visit...
queríamos visitar...
***kreea**-moosh vee-zee-**tar**...*

have you any leaflets?
tem folhetos?
*tayñ fool-**ye**-toosh*

when can we visit...?
quando podemos visitar...?
***kwañ**-doo poo-**de**-moosh vee-zee-**tar**...*

do you have a town guide?
tem um guia da cidade?
*tayñ ooñ **gee**-yuh duh see-**dad***

what day does it close?
que dia fecha?
*kuh **dee**-uh **fay**-shuh*

is it open to the public?
está aberto ao público?
*shta a-**ber**-too aoo **poo**-blee-koo*

we'd like to go to...
queríamos ir para...
***kreea**-moosh eer **pa**-ruh...*

are there any excursions?
há excursões organizadas?
*a shkoor-**soyñsh** or-ga-nee-**za**-dush*

when does it leave?
a que horas parte?
*a kee **o**-rush part*

where does it leave from?
de onde parte?
dawñd part

how much is it to get in?
quanto é a entrada?
***kwañ**-too e uh eñ-**tra**-duh*

is there a reduction for...?
fazem desconto para...?
***fa**-zayñ desh-**kawñ**-too **pa**-ruh...

children
crianças
*kree-**añ**-sush*

students
estudantes
*shtoo-**dañ**-tush*

unemployed
desempregados
*duh-zeñ-pruh-**ga**-doosh*

senior citizens
terceira idade
*tuhr-**say**-ruh ee-**dad***

PROIBIDO NADAR	NO SWIMMING
PROIBIDO MERGULHAR	NO DIVING
PERIGO	DANGER

A green flag flying at the beach means it is safe to go swimming, a yellow flag means you can swim, but it is not recommended, and red flag means it is dangerous. Beaches which meet European standards of cleanliness are allowed to fly a blue flag. Watersports are popular throughout Portugal and you can hire boats and sailboards at some resorts.

is there a quiet beach?
há uma praia sossegada?
*a **oo**-muh **pra**-yuh saw-suh-**ga**-duh*

how do I get there?
como é que se vai para lá?
*kaw-**me** kuh suh vaee pruh la*

is there a swimming pool?
há piscina?
*a **pshee**-nuh*

can we swim in the river?
pode-se nadar no rio?
*pod-suh na-**dar** noo **rree**-oo*

is the water clean?
a água é limpa?
*a **ag**-wuh e **leeñ**-puh*

is it deep?
é fundo?
*e **fooñ**-doo*

is the water cold?
a água está fria?
*a **ag**-wuh shta **free**-uh*

is it dangerous?
é perigoso?
*e pree-**gaw**-zoo*

are there currents?
há correntes?
*a koo-**rreñ**-tush*

where can we...?
onde se pode...?
awñ-duh suh pod...

windsurf
fazer windsurf
*fa-**zer** windsurf*

waterski
fazer esqui aquático
*fa-**zer** shkee a-**kwa**-tee-koo*

can I hire...?
posso alugar...
***po**-soo a-loo-**gar**...*

a beach umbrella
um chapéu de praia
*ooñ sha-**peoo** duh **pra**-yuh*

a jetski
um jet-ski
*ooñ **zhet**-skee*

33

SPORT

Tourist offices will provide information on sports activities in their area.

where can we...?
onde se pode...?
awñ-duh suh pod...

play tennis
jogar ténis
zhoo-gar te-neesh

play golf
jogar golfe
zhoo-gar golf

go swimming
nadar
nuh-dar

hire bikes
alugar bicicletas
a-loo-gar bee-see-kle-tush

go fishing
pescar
push-kar

go riding
andar a cavalo
añ-dar uh ka-va-loo

how much is it...?
quanto é...?
kwañ-too e...

per hour
por hora
poor o-ruh

per day
por dia
poor dee-uh

how do I book a court?
como se aluga um campo?
kaw-moo see a-loo-guh ooñ kañ-poo

can I hire rackets?
alugam raquetes?
a-loo-gaooñ rra-ketsh

do I need walking boots?
preciso de botas de alpinismo?
*pruh-see-zoo duh bo-tush
dal-pee-neezh-moo*

is there a football match?
há algum jogo de futebol?
a al-gooñ zhaw-goo duh foot-bol

do I need a fishing permit?
é preciso uma liçença de pesca?
e pruh-see-zoo oo-muh lee-señ-suh duh pesh-kuh

where can I get one?
onde se arranjam?
awñ-duh suh-rrañ-zhaooñ

where is there a sports shop?
onde há uma loja de artigos de desporto?
awñ-dee a oo-muh lo-zhuh dee-ar-tee-goosh duh dush-pawr-too

There are many good golf clubs in Portugal, particularly in the Algarve.

is there a golfclub near here?
há um clube de golfe aqui perto?
*a ooñ kloob duh golf **a**-kee **per**-too*

how much is a round?
quanto custa uma volta?
*kwañ-too **koosh**-tuh **oo**-muh **vol**-tuh*

do you need to be a member to play here?
é preciso ser membro para jogar?
*e pruh-**see**-zoo ser **meñ**-broo pa-ruh zhoo-**gar***

can I hire...?
pode-se alugar...?
***pod**-suh a-loo-**gar**...*

golf clubs
tacos de golfe
***ta**-koosh duh golf*

a caddie
um caddie
ooñ caddie

a buggy
um buggy
ooñ buggy

can we book tee-off times?
é possível reservar a hora de tee-off?
*e poo-**see**-vel rruh-suhr-**var** uh **o**-ruh duh tee-off*

where do I go to tee up?
onde está o primeiro tee?
***awñ**-duh shta oo pree-**may**-roo tee*

what par is this hole?
qual é o par deste buraco
*kwal e oo par desht boo-**ra**-koo*

it's in the bunker
está no bunker
shta noo bunker

qual é o seu handicap?
kwal e oo seoo handicap
what is your handicap?

o meu handicap é...
oo meoo handicap e...
my handicap is...

NIGHTLIFE – popular

Portuguese people tend to dine late and then go out afterwards. An evening out might not start until 10pm and typically involves visiting a series of bars, staying for only a short time in each one.

what is there to do at night?
o que se pode fazer à noite?
*oo kuh suh pod fa-**zer** a noyt*

which is a good bar?
onde há um bom bar por aqui?
awñ**-dee a ooñ bawñ bar poor a-**kee

which is a good disco?
qual é uma boa discoteca?
*kwal e **oo**-muh **baw**-uh deesh-koo-**te**-kuh*

where can we hear live music?
onde se pode ouvir música ao vivo?
***awñ**-duh suh pod aw-**veer moo**-zee-kuh aoo **vee**-voo*

is it expensive?
é caro?
*e **ka**-roo*

where can we hear fado/classical music?
onde se pode ouvir fado/música clássica?
***awñ**-duh suh pod aw-**veer fa**-doo/**moo**-zee-kuh **kla**-see-kuh*

where do local people go at night?
onde é que a gente de aqui vai à noite?
*awñ-**de** kuh zheñt duh-**kee** vaee a noyt*

is it a safe area?
é uma zona segura?
*e **oo**-muh **zo**-nuh suh-**goo**-ruh*

are there any concerts on?
há algum concerto por aqui?
*a al-**gooñ** kawñ-**ser**-too poor a-**kee***

quer dançar comigo?
*ker dañ-**sar** coo-**mee**-goo*
do you want to dance?

chamo-me...
*sha-**moo**-muh...*
my name is...

como se chama?
*kaw-moo suh **sha**-muh*
what's your name?

Museums are usually closed on Mondays. Opening hours vary but it is normal for museums to open from 10am to 5pm with many of them closing for lunch between noon and 2.30pm. There are many drama, dance and music summer festivals. The tourist office can give information on local events.

is there a list of cultural events?
há um guia de eventos culturais?
*a ooñ **gee**-yuh de-**veñ**-toosh kool-too-**raeesh***

what's on?
qual é o programa?
*kwal e oo pro-**gra**-muh*

when is the local festival?
quando é que são as festas da zona?
***kwañ**-doo e kuh saooñ ush **fesh**-tush duh **zaw**-nuh*

we'd like to go...
queremos ir...
***kre**-moosh eer...*

to the theatre
ao teatro
*aoo tee-**at**-roo*

to the opera
à ópera
*a **o**-puh-ruh*

to the ballet
ao ballet
*aoo ba-**le***

to a concert
a um concerto
*uh ooñ kawñ-**ser**-too*

do I need to get tickets in advance?
é preciso comprar bilhetes com antecedência?
*e pruh-**see**-zoo kawñ-**prar** beel-**yetsh** kawñ añ-tuh-suh-**deñ**-see-uh*

how much are the tickets?
quais são os preços dos bilhetes?
*kwaeesh saooñ oosh **pre**-soosh doosh beel-**yetsh***

when does the performance end?
quando acaba o espectáculo?
***kwañ**-doo a-**ka**-buh oo shpe-**ta**-koo-loo*

2 tickets...
dois bilhetes...
*doysh beel-**yetsh**...*

for tonight
para esta noite
***presh**-tuh noyt*

for tomorrow
para amanhã
*pa-ra-man-**yañ***

for 5th August
para cinco de Agosto
***pa**-ruh **seeñ**-koo duh-**gawsh**-too*

HOTEL

VACANCIES (B & B)

*Tourist offices have lists of hotels and other accommodation in their areas. You might also want to treat yourself to a stay in a **pousada** – luxurious state-run hotels which are often converted palaces, monasteries or other historic buildings.*

have you a room for tonight?
tem um quarto para esta noite?
*tayñ ooñ **kwar**-too pa-**resh**-tuh noyt*

a room	**single**	**double**	**family**
um quarto	individual	de casal	de família
*ooñ **kwar**-too*	*eeñ-dee-vee-**dwal***	*duh kuh-**zal***	*duh fa-**meel**-yuh*

	with a shower	**with a toilet**	
	com chuveiro	com casa de banho	
	*kawñ shoo-**vay**-roo*	*kawñ **ka**-suh duh **ban**-yoo*	

how much is it per night?
quanto é por noite?
***kwañ**-too e poor noyt*

is breakfast included?
inclui pequeno almoço?
*eeñ-**kloo**-ee puh-**ke**-noo al-**maw**-soo*

I booked a room
reservei um quarto
*ruh-suhr-**vay** ooñ **kwar**-too*

my name is...
chamo-me...
***sha**-moo-muh...*

I'd like to see the room
queria ver o quarto
***kree**-uh ver oo **kwar**-too*

have you anything cheaper?
não tem nada mais barato?
*naooñ tayñ **na**-duh maeesh buh-**ra**-too*

I want a room with three beds
queria um quarto com três camas
***kree**-uh ooñ **kwar**-too kawñ tresh **ka**-mush*

can I leave this in the safe?
posso deixar isto no cofre?
*po-soo day-**shar** eesh-too noo **kof**-ruh*

can I have my key, please?
queria a chave, por favor
kree-uh uh shav poor fa-vawr

are there any messages for me?
há algum recado para mim?
a al-gooñ rruh-ka-doo pruh meeñ

come in!
entre!
eñ-truh

please come back later
volte mais tarde, por favor
volt maeesh tard poor fa-vawr

I'd like breakfast in my room
queria o pequeno almoço no quarto
kree-uh oo puh-ke-noo al-maw-soo noo kwar-too

please bring...
por favor traga-me...
poor fa-vawr tra-ga-muh...

toilet paper
papel higiénico
pa-pel ee-zhee-e-nee-koo

soap
sabonete
sa-boo-net

clean towels
toalhas limpas
twal-yush leeñ-push

a glass
um copo
ooñ ko-poo

could you clean...?
podia limpar...?
poo-dee-uh leeñ-par...

my room
o meu quarto
oo meoo kwar-too

the bath
a banheira
uh ban-yay-ruh

please call me...
podia-me chamar...
poo-dee-a-muh sha-mar...

at 8 o'clock
às oito horas
azh oy-too o-rush

do you have a laundry service?
tem serviço de lavandaria?
tayñ suhr-vee-soo duh la-vañ-duh-reea

we're leaving tomorrow
vamos embora amanhã
va-moosh eñ-bo-ra-man-yañ

could you prepare the bill?
faça a conta, por favor
fa-suh uh kawñ-tuh poor fa-vawr

SELF-CATERING

The voltage in Portugal is 220. Plugs have two round pins and you should take an adaptor if you plan to take any electrical appliances with you.

which is the key for this door?
qual é a chave desta porta?
*kwal e uh shav **desh**-tuh **por**-tuh*

please show us how this works
podia mostrar-me como é que isto funciona?
*poo-**dee**-a moosh-**trar**-muh kaw-**me**-keesh-too fooñ-see-**yaw**-nuh*

how does ... work?
como é que o/a ... trabalha?
*kaw-**me** kee oo/uh...tra-**bal**-yuh*

the waterheater
o esquentador
*oo shkeñ-ta-**dawr***

the washing machine
a máquina de lavar roupa
*uh **ma**-kee-nuh duh luh-**var rraw**-puh*

the cooker
o fogão
*oo foo-**gaooñ***

who do I contact if there are any problems?
quem é que devo contactar no caso de haver problemas?
*kayñ e kuh **de**-voo kawñ-tak-**tar** noo **ka**-zoo da-**ver** proo-**ble**-mush*

we need extra...
precisamos de mais...
*pruh-see-**za**-moosh de maeesh...*

cutlery
talheres
*tal-**ye**-rush*

sheets
lençóis
*leñ-**soysh***

the gas has run out
acabou-se o gás
*a-kuh-**baws** oo gazh*

what do I do?
o que devo fazer?
*o kuh **de**-voo fa-**zer***

where are the fuses?
onde estão os fusíveis?
***awñ**-duh shtaooñ oosh foo-**zee**-vaysh*

where do I put out the rubbish?
onde é que se põe o lixo?
*awñ-**de** kuh suh poyñ oo **lee**-shoo*

CAMPING & CARAVANNING

*There are many sites along the coast, fewer in the inland areas.
Camping outside approved sites is possible except in the Algarve
where this is strictly prohibited. If towing a caravan or trailer you
need an international camping carnet available from the Caravan
Club.*

we're looking for a campsite
procuramos um parque de campismo
*pro-koo-**ra**-moosh ooñ park duh kañ-**peezh**-moo*

have you a list of campsites?
tem uma lista de parques de campismo?
*tayñ **oo**-muh **leesh**-tuh duh **par**-kush duh kañ-**peezh**-moo*

where is the campsite?
onde é o parque de campismo?
***awñ**-dee e oo park duh kañ-**peezh**-moo*

have you any vacancies?
tem lugares vagos?
*tayñ loo-**ga**-rush **va**-goosh*

how much is it per night?
quanto custa por noite?
***kwañ**-too **koosh**-tuh poor noyt*

we'd like to stay for ... nights
gostaríamos de ficar ... noites
*goosh-ta-**reea**-moosh duh fee-**kar** ... noytsh*

is the campsite near the beach?
o parque de campismo fica perto da praia?
*oo park duh kañ-**peezh**-moo **fee**-kuh **per**-too duh **pra**-yuh*

do you have a more sheltered site?
não tem um lugar mais abrigado?
*naooñ tayñ ooñ loo-**gar** maeesh uh-bree-**ga**-doo*

it is very muddy here
há muita lama aqui
*a **mweeñ**-tuh **la**-muh uh-**kee***

is there another site?
há outro parque?
*a **aw**-troo park*

is there a shop on the site?
há alguma loja no parque?
*a al-**goo**-muh **lo**-zhuh noo park*

can we camp here?
podemos acampar aqui?
*poo-**de**-moosh a-kañ-**par** a-**kee***

can we park our caravan here?
podemos estacionar a nossa caravana aqui?
*poo-**de**-moosh shtas-yoo-**nar** uh **no**-suh
ka-ruh-**va**-nuh uh-**kee***

for the night
para passar a noite
***pa**-ruh pa-**sar** uh noyt*

41

CHILDREN

Children are welcome in Portuguese restaurants and you can order children's portions or half portions.

a child's ticket
um bilhete de criança
*ooñ beel-**yet** duh kree-**añ**-suh*

is there a reduction for children?
fazem descontos para crianças?
***fa**-zayñ dush-**kawñ**-toosh **pa**-ruh kree-**añ**-sush*

do you have a children's menu?
tem uma ementa para crianças?
*tayñ **oo**-muh ee-**meñ**-tuh **pa**-ruh kree-**añ**-sush*

do you have...?	**a high chair**	**a cot**
tem...?	uma cadeira-de-bebé	um berço
tayñ...	***oo**-muh kuh-**day**-ruh duh be-**be***	*ooñ **ber**-soo*

is it ok to bring children here?
é possível trazer as crianças?
*e poo-**see**-vel tra-**zer** ush kree-**añ**-sush*

what is there for children to do?
o que há para as crianças fazerem?
*oo kee a **pa**-ruh ush kree-**añ**-sush fa-**ze**-rayñ*

is it safe for children?
pode-se dar às crianças?
***pod**-suh dar azh kree-**añ**-sush*

is it dangerous?
é perigoso?
*e pree-**gaw**-zoo*

I have two children
tenho duas crianças
***tayn**-yoo **doo**-ush kree-**añ**-sush*

he/she is 10 years old
ele/ela tem dez anos
*el/ela tayñ dezh **uh**-noosh*

do you have children?
tem filhos?
*tayñ **feel**-yoosh*

SPECIAL NEEDS

Tourist offices can supply a list of hotels with facilities for the disabled. Some campsites and youth hostels provide special facilities.

is it possible to visit ... with a wheelchair?
é possível visitar ... com uma cadeira de rodas?
*e poo-**see**-vel vee-zee-**tar** ... kawñ **oo**-muh ka-**day**-ruh duh **rro**-dush*

do you have toilets for the disabled?
tem casa de banho para deficientes?
*tayñ **ka**-zuh duh **ban**-yoo **pa**-ruh duh-fee-see-**eñtsh***

I need a bedroom on the ground floor
preciso um quarto no rés-do-chão
*pruh-**see**-zoo ooñ **kwar**-too noo rrezh-doo-**shaooñ***

is there a lift?
há elevador?
*a ee-luh-va-**dawr***

where is the lift?
onde é o elevador?
awñ**-dee e oo ee-luh-va-**dawr

I can't walk far
não posso andar muito
*naooñ **po**-soo añ-**dar mweeñ**-too*

are there many steps?
há muitos degraus?
*a **mweeñ**-toosh duh-**gra**-oosh*

is there an entrance for wheelchairs?
há uma entrada para cadeiras de rodas?
*a **oo**-muh eñ-**tra**-duh **pa**-ruh ka-**day**-rush duh **rro**-dush*

can I travel on this train with a wheelchair?
posso viajar neste comboio com cadeira de rodas?
***po**-soo veea-**zhar** nesht kawñ-**bo**-yoo kawñ ka-**day**-ruh duh **rro**-dush*

is there a reduction for the disabled?
há desconto para deficientes?
*a dush-**kawñ**-too **pa**-ruh duh-fee-see-**eñtsh***

EXCHANGE VISITORS

*These phrases are intended for families hosting Portuguese-speaking visitors. We have used the familiar **tu** form.*

what would you like for breakfast?
o que queres para o pequeno almoço?
*oo kuh **ke**-rush **pa**-ruh oo puh-**ke**-noo al-**maw**-soo*

do you eat...?
comes...?
***ko**-mush...*

what would you like to eat?
o que queres comer?
*oo kuh **ke**-rush koo-**mer***

what would you like to drink?
o que queres beber?
*oo kuh **ke**-rush buh-**ber***

did you sleep well?
dormiste bem?
*door-**meesh**-tuh bayñ*

would you like to take a shower?
queres tomar banho?
***ke**-rush **too**-mar **ban**-yoo*

what would you like to do today?
o que queres fazer hoje?
*oo kuh **ke**-rush fa-**zer** awzh*

would you like to go shopping?
queres ir às compras?
***ke**-ruh-sheer azh **kawñ**-prush*

I will pick you up at...
vou-te buscar às...
***vaw**-tuh **boosh**-kar azh...*

did you enjoy yourself?
divertiste-te?
*dee-vuhr-**teesh**-tuh-tuh*

take care
tem cuidado
*tayñ kwee-**da**-doo*

please be back by...
volta antes de...
***vol**-tuh **añ**-tush duh...*

we'll be in bed when you get back
estaremos na cama quando voltares
*shta-**re**-moosh nuh **ka**-muh **kwañ**-doo vol-**ta**-rush*

EXCHANGE VISITORS

These phrases are intended for those people staying with Portuguese-speaking families.

I like...
gosto de....
gosh-too duh...

I don't like...
não gosto de...
naooñ gosh-too duh...

that was delicious
estava uma delícia
shta-vuh oo-muh duh-lee-see-uh

thank you very much
muito obrigado(da)
mweeñ-too o-bree-ga-doo(-duh)

may I phone home?
posso telefonar para casa?
po-soo tuh-luh-foo-nar pa-ruh ka-suh

may I make a local call?
posso fazer uma chamada local?
po-soo fa-zer oo-muh sha-ma-duh loo-kal

can I have a key?
podia dar-me uma chave?
poo-dee-uh dar-muh oo-muh shav

can you take me by car?
podia-me levar de carro?
poo-dee-uh-muh luh-var duh ka-rroo

can I borrow...?
podia-me emprestar...?
poo-dee-uh-muh eñ-prush-tar...

an iron
um ferro
ooñ fe-rroo

a hairdryer
um secador de cabelo
ooñ se-ka-dawr duh ka-be-loo

what time do you get up?
a que horas te levantas?
a kee o-rush tuh luh-vañ-tush

please would you call me at...
podia-me chamar às...
poo-dee-uh-muh shuh-mar azh...

who are you staying with?
com quem estás a ficar?
kawñ kayñ shtas uh fee-kar

I'm staying with...
estou a ficar na casa de...
shtaw uh fee-kar nuh ka-suh duh...

thanks for everything
obrigado(da) por tudo
o-bree-ga-doo(-duh) poor too-doo

I've had a great time
diverti-me imenso
dee-vuhr-tee-muh ee-meñ-soo

PROBLEMS

can you help me, please?
pode-me ajudar, por favor?
*pod-muh-zhoo-**dar** poor fa-**vawr***

I don't speak Portuguese
não falo português
*naooñ **fa**-loo poor-too-**gesh***

do you speak English?
fala inglês?
fa**-luh eeñ-**glesh

does anyone speak English?
há alguém que fale inglês?
*a al-**gayñ** kuh fal eeñ-**glesh***

I'm lost
perdi-me
*puhr-**deem***

how do I get to...?
como se vai para...?
***kaw**-moo suh vaee **pa**-ruh...*

I'm late
estou atrasado(da)
*shtaw a-tra-**za**-doo(-duh)*

I need to get to...
preciso de ir a...
*pruh-**see**-zoo deer uh...*

I've missed...
perdi...
*puhr-**dee**...*

my plane
o avião
*oo a-vee-**aooñ***

my connection
a minha ligação
*uh **meen**-yuh lee-ga-**saooñ***

I've lost...
perdi...
*puhr-**dee**...*

my wallet
o porta-moedas
*oo por-ta-**mwe**-dush*

my passport
o passaporte
*o pa-sa-**port***

my luggage has not arrived
a minha bagagem não chegou
*un **meen**-yuh ba-**ga**-zhayñ naooñ shuh-**gaw***

I've left my bag in...
deixei a mala em...
*day-**shay** uh **ma**-luh ayñ...*

on the coach
no autocarro
*noo o-to-**ka**-rroo*

is there a lost property office?
há uma secção de perdidos e achados?
*a **oo**-muh sek-**saooñ** duh puhr-**dee**-doosh ee a-**sha**-doosh*

leave me alone!
deixe-me em paz!
***daysh**-mayñ pazh*

go away!
vá-se embora!
*va-señ-**bo**-ruh*

46

the light
a luz
a loozh

the air conditioning
o ar condicionado
*oo ar kawñ-dees-yoo-**na**-doo*

...doesn't work
...não trabalha
*...naooñ tra-**bal**-yuh*

the room is dirty
o quarto está sujo
*oo **kwar**-too shta **soo**-zhoo*

the bath is dirty
a banheira está suja
*uh ban-**yay**-ruh shta **soo**-zhuh*

there is no...
não há...
naooñ a...

hot water
água quente
***ag**-wuh keñt*

toilet paper
papel higiénico
*pa-**pel** ee-zhee-**e**-nee-koo*

it is too noisy
há muito ruído
*a **mweeñ**-too **rrwee**-doo*

it is too small
é muito pequeno
*e **mweeñ**-too puh-**ke**-noo*

this isn't what I ordered
isto não é o que eu pedi
eesh**-too naooñ e oo kee eoo puh-**dee

I want to complain
quero apresentar uma queixa
***ke**-roo a-pruh-señ-**tar oo**-muh **kay**-shuh*

I want my money back
quero um reembolso
*ke-roo ooñ rree-eñ-**bawl**-soo*

we've been waiting for a very long time
estamos à espera há muito tempo
***shta**-moosh a **shpe**-ruh a **mweeñ**-too **teñ**-poo*

there is a mistake
há um erro
*a ooñ **e**-rroo*

this is broken
isto está partido
***eesh**-too shta par-**tee**-doo*

can you repair it?
pode arranjá-lo?
*pod a-rrañ-**zha**-loo*

EMERGENCIES

POLÍCIA	POLICE
BOMBEIROS	FIRE BRIGADE
BANCO DO HOSPITAL	CASUALTY DEPARTMENT

POLICE, AMBULANCE, FIRE   *112*

Dial 112 and state which service you require.

help!
socorro!
soo-**kaw**-rroo

can you help me?
pode-me ajudar?
pod-muh-zhoo-**dar**

there's been an accident
houve um acidente
awv ooñ a-see-**deñt**

someone is injured
há um ferido
a ooñ fuh-**ree**-doo

call...
chame...
sham...

the police
a polícia
uh poo-**lees**-yuh

an ambulance
uma ambulância
oo-mañ-boo-**lañ**-see-yuh

he was driving too fast
ele estava a conduzir rápido demais
el **shta**-vuh uh kawñ-doo-**zeer** rra-pee-doo duh-**maeesh**

where's the police station?
onde é a esquadra?
awñ-dee e uh **shkwa**-druh

the insurance company requires me to report it
a companhia de seguros requer que eu o participe
a kawñ-pan-**yee**-uh duh suh-**goo**-roosh rruh-**ker** kee eoo oo par-tee-**seep**

EMERGENCIES

I've been robbed
fui roubado(da)
*fooee rraw-**ba**-doo(-duh)*

I've been attacked
fui agredido(da)
*fooee a-gruh-**dee**-doo(-duh)*

I've been raped
violaram-me
*veeoo-**la**-raooñ-muh*

my car has been broken into
assaltaram-me o carro
*a-sal-**ta**-raooñ-muh oo **ka**-rroo*

my car has been stolen
roubaram-me o carro
*rraw-**ba**-raooñ-muh oo **ka**-rroo*

that man keeps following me
aquele homem está me a seguir
*a-**kel o**-mayñ **shta**-muh suh-**geer***

how much is the fine?
quanto é a multa?
***kwañ**-too e uh **mool**-tuh*

I don't have enough
não tenho o suficiente
*naooñ **tayn**-yoo oo soo-fees-**yeñt***

can I pay at the police station?
posso pagar na esquadra?
***po**-soo pa-**gar** nuh **shkwa**-druh*

I would like to phone my embassy
gostava de telefonar à minha embaixada
*goosh-**ta**-vuh duh tuh-luh-foo-**nar** a **meen**-yuh eñ-baee-**sha**-duh*

where is the British Consulate?
onde é que fica o consulado britânico?
*awñ-**de** kuh **fee**-kuh oo kawñ-soo-**la**-doo bree-**tañ**-nee-koo*

I have no money
não tenho dinheiro nenhum
*naooñ **tayn**-yoo deen-**yay**-roo nayn-**yooñ***

vamos lá ter
***va**-moosh la ter*
we're on our way

49

HEALTH

FARMÁCIA	PHARMACY
HOSPITAL	HOSPITAL
BANCO DO HOSPITAL	ACCIDENT AND EMERGENCY DEPT

EU citizens are entitled to free emergency care in Portugal. You should take with you form E111, completed and stamped at a post office in the UK before your trip. However you will need to take out a medical insurance policy to cover non-emergency treatment. Pharmacies will be able to provide advice on any health matters and deal with minor problems.

have you something for...?
tem algo para...?
*tayñ **al**-goo **pa**-ruh...*

car sickness
o enjoo
*oo eñ-**zhaw**-oo*

diarrhoea
a diarreia
*uh deea-**rray**-uh*

is it safe for children to take?
pode-se dar às crianças?
*pod-suh dar azh kree-**añ**-sush*

I don't feel well
não me sinto bem
*naooñ muh **seen**-too bayñ*

I need a doctor
preciso de um médico
*pruh-**see**-zoo dooñ **me**-dee-koo*

I'm taking these drugs
estou a tomar estes medicamentos
*shtaw a too-**mar esh**-tush muh-dee-ka-**meñ**-toosh*

my son/daughter is ill
o meu filho/a minha filha está doente
*oo meoo **feel**-yoo/uh **meen**-yuh feel-yuh shta doo-**eñt***

he/she has a temperature
ele/ela tem febre
*el/**e**-la tayñ **feb**-ruh*

I have high blood pressure
tenho a tensão alta
***tayn**-yoo uh teñ-**saooñ al**-tuh*

I'm pregnant
estou grávida
*shtaw **gra**-vee-duh*

I'm on the pill
tomo a pílula
***to**-moo uh **pee**-loo-luh*

I'm allergic to penicillin
sou alérgico(ca) à penicilina
*saw a-**ler**-zhee-koo(-kuh) a pe-nee-see-**lee**-nuh*

my blood group is...
o meu grupo sanguíneo é...
*oo meoo **groo**-poo sañ-**gwee**-neeoo e...*

I'm breastfeeding
estou a amamentar
*shtaw uh a-ma-meñ-**tar***

is it safe to take?
tem contra-indicações?
*tayñ kawñ-tra-eeñ-dee-ka-**soyñsh***

will he/she have to go to hospital?
tem que ir para o hospital?
*tayñ keer **pa**-ruh oo osh-pee-**tal***

I need to go to casualty
preciso de ir às urgências
*pruh-**see**-zoo deer azh oor-**zheñ**-see-ush*

where is the hospital?
onde é o hospital?
awñ**-dee e oo osh-pee-**tal

when are visiting hours?
quais são as horas de visita?
*kwaeesh saooñ ush **o**-rush duh vee-**zee**-tuh*

which ward?
qual é a enfermaria?
*kwal e uh eñ-fuhr-ma-**ree**-yuh*

I need to see the dentist
preciso de um dentista
*pruh-**see**-zoo dooñ deñ-**teesh**-tuh*

I have toothache
tenho uma dor de dentes
***tayn**-yoo **oo**-muh dawr duh dentsh*

the filling has come out
caíu-me o chumbo
*ka-**eeoo**-muh oo **shooñ**-boo*

it hurts
dói-me
***doy**-muh*

my dentures are broken
a dentadura está partida
*uh deñ-ta-**doo**-ruh shta par-**tee**-duh*

can you repair them?
podia reparápor-la?
*poo-**dee**-uh rruh-pa-**ra**-luh*

I have an abscess
tenho um abcesso
***tayn**-yoo ooñ ab-**se**-soo*

BUSINESS

Office hours vary but most offices open at 9am, have a lunch hour (usually from 1 to 3pm) and close at 6 or 7 in the evening. Government offices are open to the public from 9am to 1pm.

I'm...
sou...
saw...

here's my card
aqui tem o meu cartão
a-kee tayñ oo meoo kar-taooñ

I'm from Jones Ltd
sou de Jones Limitada
saw duh Jones lee-mee-ta-duh

I'd like to arrange a meeting with Mr/Ms...
gostaria de ter uma reunião com o Senhor/a Senhora...
goosh-ta-ree-yuh duh ter oo-muh rreoo-nee-aooñ kawñ oo suhn-yawr/uh suhn-yaw-ruh...

can we meet at a restaurant?
podíamos-nos encontrar num restaurante?
poo-dee-uh-moosh nooz eñ-kawñ-trar nooñ rrush-to-rañt

I will confirm by fax
confirmarei por fax
kawñ-feer-ma-ray poor faks

I'm staying at Hotel...
estou no Hotel...
shtaw noo o-tel...

how do I get to your office?
como se vai ao seu escritório?
kaw-moo suh vaee aoo seoo shkree-to-reeoo

here is some information about my company
aqui tem informação sobre a minha empresa
a-kee tayñ eeñ-foor-muh-saooñ saw-bruh uh meen-yuh eñ-pre-zuh

52

I have an appointment with...
tenho um encontro com...
tayn-yoo ooñ eñ-**kawñ**-troo kawñ...

at ... o'clock
às ... horas
*azh ... **o**-rush*

I'm delighted to meet you
prazer em conhecê-lo(la)
*pra-**zer** ayñ kawñ-yuh-**se**-loo(-luh)*

my Portuguese isn't very good
não falo muito bem português
*naooñ **fa**-loo **mweeñ**-too bayñ poor-too-**gesh***

what is the name of the managing director?
como é que se chama o director geral/a directora geral?
*kaw-**me** kuh suh **sha**-muh oo dee-rek-**tawr** zhuh-**ral**/
a dee-rek-**taw**-ruh zhuh-**ral***

I would like some information about the company
queria informação sobre a companhia
***kree**-uh eeñ-foor-ma-**saooñ saw**-bruh uh kawñ-pan-**yee**-uh*

do you have a press office?
tem um departamento de imprensa?
*tayñ ooñ duh-puhr-ta-**meñ**-too deeñ-preñ-suh*

I need an interpreter
preciso de um intérprete
*pruh-**see**-zoo dooñ eeñ-**ter**-pruh-tuh*

can you photocopy this for me?
podia fotocopiar-me isto?
*poo-**dee**-uh fo-to-koo-pee-yar-**meesh**-too*

is there a business centre?
há um centro de negócios?
*a ooñ **señ**-troo duh nuh-**gos**-yoosh*

tem encontro marcado?
*tayñ eñ-**kawñ**-troo mar-**ka**-doo?*
do you have an appointment?

PHONING

Coin-operated can be quite hard to find, but card-operated machines are becoming much more common – you can buy phonecards from post offices, newsstands and tobacconists. To call abroad, dial 00 before the country code. The country code for Britain is 44.

a phonecard
um cartão credifone
*ooñ kar-**taooñ** kre-dee-**fon***

for 50/100 units
de 50/100 impulsos
*duh seen-**kweñ**-tuh/sayñ eeñ-**pool**-soosh*

I want to make a phone call
quero fazer uma chamada telefónica
***ke**-roo fa-**zer oo**-muh sha-**ma**-duh tuh-luh-**fo**-nee-kuh*

I want to make a reverse charge call
quero fazer uma chamada a cobrar no destinatário
***ke**-roo fa-**zer oo**-muh sha-**ma**-duh a koo-**brar** noo dush-tee-na-**ta**-ree-yoo*

can I speak to...?
posso falar com...?
***po**-soo fa-**lar** kawñ...*

this is...
aqui fala...
*a-**kee fa**-luh...*

Senhor Lopes, please
o Senhor Lopes, por favor
*oo suhn-**yawr Lop**-sh poor fa-**vawr***

I'll call back later
chamo mais tarde
sha-moo maeesh tard

can you give me an outside line, please
dê-me uma linha, por favor
de**-muh **oo**-muh **leen**-yuh poor fa-**vawr

estou/alô/sim
*shtaw/a-**law**/seeñ*
hello

quem fala?
*kayñ **fa**-luh*
who is calling?

está impedido
shta eeñ-puh-dee-doo
it's engaged

por favor, volte a tentar mais tarde
*poor fa-**vawr** volt uh teñ-**tar** maeesh tard*
please try again later

FAXING/E-MAIL

I want to send a fax
queria mandar um fax
kree-uh mañ-dar ooñ faks

what's your fax number?
qual é o seu número de fax?
kwal e oo seoo noo-muh-roo duh faks

please resend your fax
por favor repita o fax
poor fa-vawr rruh-pee-tuh oo faks

the fax is engaged
o fax está impedido
oo faks shta eeñ-puh-dee-doo

can I send a fax from here?
posso mandar um fax daqui?
po-soo mañ-dar ooñ faks da-kee

did you get my fax?
recebeu o meu fax?
rruh-suh-beoo oo meoo faks

I want to send an e-mail
queria mandar um e-mail
kree-uh mañ-dar ooñ e-mail

what's your e-mail address?
qual é o seu endereço de correio electrónico?
kwal e oo seoo eñ-dre-soo duh koo-rray-oo ee-le-tro-nee-koo

my e-mail address is...
o meu endereço de correio electrónico é...
oo meoo eñ-dre-soo duh koo-rray-oo ee-le-tro-nee-koo e...

did you get my e-mail?
recebeu o meu e-mail?
ruh-suh-beoo oo meoo e-mail

do you have a fax?
tem fax?
tayñ faks

I can't read it
é ilegível
e ee-luh-zhee-vel

NUMBERS

0	**zero** *ze-roo*	
1	**um (uma)** *ooñ (oo-muh)*	
2	**dois (duas)** *doysh (doo-ush)*	
3	**três** *tresh*	
4	**quatro** *kwa-troo*	
5	**cinco** *seeñ-koo*	
6	**seis** *saysh*	
7	**sete** *set*	
8	**oito** *oy-too*	
9	**nove** *nov*	
10	**dez** *desh*	
11	**onze** *awñz*	
12	**doze** *dawz*	
13	**treze** *trez*	
14	**catorze** *ka-tawrz*	
15	**quinze** *keeñz*	
16	**dezasseis** *dzuh-saysh*	
17	**dezassete** *dzuh-set*	
18	**dezoito** *dzoy-too*	
19	**dezanove** *dzuh-nov*	
20	**vinte** *veent*	
21	**vinte e um** *veeñ-tee-ooñ*	
22	**vinte e dois** *veeñ-tee-doysh*	
30	**trinta** *treeñ-tuh*	
40	**quarenta** *kwa-reñ-tuh*	
50	**cinquenta** *seeñ-kweñ-tuh*	
60	**sessenta** *suh-señ-tuh*	
70	**setenta** *suh-teñ-tuh*	
80	**oitenta** *oy-teñ-tuh*	
90	**noventa** *noo-veñ-tuh*	
100	**cem / cento** *sayñ / señ-too*	
110	**cento e dez** *señ-too ee desh*	
200	**duzentos** *doo-zeñ-toosh*	
500	**quinhentos** *keen-yeñ-toosh*	
1000	**mil** *meel*	
million	**um milhão** *ooñ meel-yaooñ*	

1st	**primeiro** *pree-may-roo*
2nd	**segundo** *suh-gooñ-doo*
3rd	**terceiro** *tuhr-say-roo*
4th	**quarto** *kwar-too*
5th	**quinto** *keeñ-too*
6th	**sexto** *saysh-too*
7th	**sétimo** *se-tee-moo*
8th	**oitavo** *oy-ta-voo*
9th	**nono** *naw-noo*
10th	**décimo** *de-see-moo*

DAYS & MONTHS

JANEIRO	JANUARY
FEVEREIRO	FEBRUARY
MARÇO	MARCH
ABRIL	APRIL
MAIO	MAY
JUNHO	JUNE
JULHO	JULY
AGOSTO	AUGUST
SETEMBRO	SEPTEMBER
OUTUBRO	OCTOBER
NOVEMBRO	NOVEMBER
DEZEMBRO	DECEMBER

SEGUNDA-FEIRA	MONDAY
TERÇA-FEIRA	TUESDAY
QUARTA-FEIRA	WEDNESDAY
QUINTA-FEIRA	THURSDAY
SEXTA-FEIRA	FRIDAY
SÁBADO	SATURDAY
DOMINGO	SUNDAY

what's the date?
qual é a data?
*kwal e uh **da**-tuh*

which day?
que dia?
*kuh **dee**-uh*

which month?
que mês?
kuh mesh

March 5th
cinco de Março
***seeñ**-koo duh **mar**-soo*

July 6th
seis de Julho
*saysh duh **zhool**-yoo*

on Saturday
no sábado
*noo **sa**-ba-doo*

on Saturdays
aos sábados
*aoosh **sa**-ba-doosh*

every Saturday
todos os sábados
***taw**-doosh oosh **sa**-ba-doosh*

this Saturday
este sábado
*esht **sa**-ba-doo*

next Saturday
o próximo sábado
*oo **pro**-see-moo **sa**-ba-doo*

last Saturday
o sábado passado
*o **sa**-ba-doo pa-**sa**-doo*

next week
a semana que vem
*uh suh-**ma**-nuh kuh vayñ*

last month
o mês passado
*oo mesh pa-**sa**-doo*

please can you confirm the date?
podia confirmar a data?
*poo-**dee**-uh kawñ-feer-**mar** uh **da**-tuh*

TIME

Note that throughout Europe the 24-hour clock is used much more widely than in the UK.

what time is it, please?
que horas são, por favor?
*kee **o**-rush saooñ poor fa-**vawr***

am
da manhã
*duh man-**yañ***

pm
da tarde
duh tard

it's 1 o'clock
é uma hora
*e **oo**-muh **o**-ruh*

it's 2/3 o'clock
são duas/três horas
*saooñ **doo**-ush/tresh **o**-rush*

it's half past 8
são oito e meia
*saooñ **oy**-too ee **may**-uh*

it is half past 10
são dez e meia
*saooñ desh ee **may**-uh*

in an hour
dentro de uma hora
***deñ**-troo dee **oo**-muh **o**-ruh*

in half an hour
dentro de meia hora
***deñ**-troo duh **may**-uh **o**-ruh*

a quarter of an hour
um quarto de hora
*ooñ **kwar**-too **do**-ruh*

three quarters of an hour
três quartos de hora
*tresh **kwar**-toosh **do**-ruh*

until 8 o'clock
até às oito
*a-**te** azh **oy**-too*

until 4 o'clock
até às quatro
*a-**te** azh **kwa**-troo*

at 10 am
às dez horas
*azh dez **o**-rush*

at 2200
às vinte e duas horas
*azh **veeñ**-tee **doo**-ush **o**-rush*

at midday
ao meio-dia
*aoo may-oo-**dee**-uh*

at midnight
à meia-noite
*a may-uh-**noyt***

soon
em breve
ayñ brev

later
mais tarde
maeesh tard

FOOD

ORDERING DRINKS

Drinks are served either **fresca** (from the fridge) or **natural** (at room temperature. Café-type places serve meals throughout the day.

a black coffee	**a white coffee**	**2 white coffees**
um café	um café com leite	dois cafés com leite
*ooñ ka-**fe***	*ooñ ka-**fe** kawñ layt*	*doysh ka-**fes** kawñ layt*

a tea	**with milk**	**with lemon**
um chá	com leite	com limão
ooñ sha	*kawñ layt*	*kawñ lee-**maooñ***

a lager	**large**	**small**
uma cerveja	grande	pequeno
***oo**-muh suhr-**vay**-shuh*	***grañ**-duh*	*puh-**ke**-noo*

a bottle of mineral water
uma garrafa de água mineral
oo**-muh ga-**rra**-fuh dag-wuh mee-nuh-**ral

sparkling	**still**
com gás	sem gás
kawñ gash	*sayñ gash*

the wine list, please
a lista de vinhos, por favor
*uh **leesh**-tuh duh **veen**-yoosh poor fa-**vawr***

a glass or red wine	**a glass of white wine**
um copo de vinho tinto	um copo de vinho branco
*ooñ **ko**-poo duh **veen**-yoo teeñ-too*	*ooñ **ko**-poo duh **veen**-yoo **brañ**-koo*

a bottle of wine	**red**	**white**
uma garrafa du vinho	tinto	branco
***oo**-muh guh-**rra**-fuh duh **veen**-yoo*	***teeñ**-too*	***brañ**-koo*

another bottle, please
mais uma garrafa, por favor
*maeesh **oo**-muh ga-**rra**-fuh poor fa-**vawr***

would you like a drink?	**what will you have?**
quer uma bebida?	o que quer tomar?
*ker **oo**-muh buh-**bee**-duh*	*o kuh ker too-**mar***

ORDERING FOOD

where is there a good local restaurant?
onde há um bom restaurante local?
awñ-dee a ooñ bawñ rrush-to-rant loo-kal

I'd like to book a table
queria reservar uma mesa
kree-uh ruh-zuhr-var oo-muh me-zuh

for ... people
para ... pessoas
pa-ruh ... puh-saw-ush

for tonight
para esta noite
presh-tuh noyt

at 8 pm
às oito horas
ash oy-too o-rush

the menu, please
a ementa, por favor
uh ee-men-tuh poor fa-vawr

is there a dish of the day?
há um prato do dia?
a ooñ pra-too doo dee-uh

have you a set-price menu?
tem a ementa do dia?
tayñ uh ee-men-tuh doo dee-uh

I'll have this
quero isto
ke-roo eesh-too

what do you recommend?
o que recomenda?
oo kuh ruh-koo-meñ-duh

I don't eat meat
ñao como carne
naooñ kaw-moo karn

do you have any vegetarian dishes?
tem algum prato vegetariano?
tayñ al-gooñ pra-too vuh-zhuh-tuh-ree-a-noo

excuse me!
faz favor!
fash fa-vawr

please bring...
traga...
tra-guh...

more bread
mais pão
maeesh paooñ

more water
mais água
maeesh ag-wuh

the bill, please
a conta, por favor
uh kawn-tuh poor fa-vawr

bom apetite!
bawñ a-puh-teet
enjoy your meal!

PORTUGUESE FOOD

Portuguese cuisine is varied and quite distinctive, despite the size of the country and its proximity to Spain. Anyone expecting to find an extension of Spanish food with **paellas** and suchlike, will be surprised to discover that Portuguese food is very different.

Every province has its own gastronomic specialities, according to its geographical characteristics, but there are various national culinary preferences found throughout Portugal, such as the use of **bacalhau** (salt cod) under many delicious guises, as well as **peixe** (fish) and **marisco** (shellfish), especially along the extensive coastline. Pork is the most popular meat in Portugal, fresh or cured, in the form of the excellent **presunto** (cured ham) and many kinds of spicy **chouriços** (smoked spicy sausages) which are delicious both raw or cooked, either to enhance the flavour of countless dishes or as the main ingredient. Lamb, kid, poultry and game are also very common all over the country. Garlic and fragrant fresh coriander are essential ingredients of many Portuguese dishes. Alongside olive oil and other vegetable oils, lard is widely used as well as butter.

However, the taste of olive oil (**azeite**) is what predominates in many dishes, from soups to salads and even delicious spicy cakes. Many people add a spoonful of olive oil to their vegetable soups, at the table, and poached fish (**peixe cozido**) or salt cod, as well as potatoes and other vegetables accompanying them, are also seasoned with lashings of olive oil. The cruet-stand (**galheteiro**) will automatically be brought to the table for you to use as liberally as you like. Portugal's terrain and climate are ideal for growing olive trees, especially along the Douro, Trás-os-Montes, Beira Baixa, the Ribatejo and, mainly, the Alentejo. The number of olive groves is expanding and the oil is extracted using the latest techniques, with excellent results.

The Portuguese are very fond of bread and bake a great variety of loaves, generally made with mixed flours (wheat, rye and maize). Bread is served at the table, both at home and in restaurants. Many national specialities are actually based on **açordas** (cooked bread) served in place of potatoes or rice, or as a main dish when mixed with all sorts of seafood or meats and seasoned with herbs and garlic. The result is delicious even if the appearance of such dishes is not too sophisticated.

PORTUGUESE FOOD

Generally speaking food in Portugal is wholesome, satisfying and full of flavour. The Portuguese eat well and serve very generous portions. The only light meal is **pequeno almoço** (breakfast) normally consisting of white coffee, **pão** (bread) or **torradas** (toast) and butter, and honey or jam. Mid-morning is time for **um croissant com fiambre** (a ham-filled croissant) or **um bolo e um café** (a cake and coffee).

Lunch and dinner (**almoço** and **jantar**) may be similar although habits are changing. Nowadays many busy people in towns have no time to go home for lunch as they used to and adopt a lighter diet, choosing a lunch of **sopa e um papo-seco** (soup and a roll) followed perhaps by **sobremesa** (dessert) and a **café** (coffee) which they may eat in one of the cafeterias and pâtisseries found on most streets. Others, however, continue to sit down for a proper, long lunch, when they meet friends or business partners. This meal, like dinner, often consists of soup – the Portuguese are very partial to their wonderful soups – or another **entrada** (starter) and **prato principal** (main dish) with fish or meat. This main dish will probably contain vegetables in some form and rice or potatoes, but there will also be a salad option. **Sobremesa** (dessert) generally follows. This may be cheese and biscuits, fruit salad, fresh fruit, a pudding or ice-cream, followed by the inevitable **bica** (strong black coffee). Some may take a local **bagaceira** or **aguardente** (brandy), with their coffee as a **digestivo** (digestive).

Mid-afternoon is again a time for snacking on **bolos** (cakes). Portugal has a wealth of delicious cakes based mainly on egg yolks and sugar. The older generation may sit down for a **merenda** or **lanche** (afternoon snack consisting of pale plain tea accompanied by cakes or buttered toast).

MAIN CHARACTERISTICS OF THE REGIONS

Portugal can be divided into three main regions (North, Central and South) plus the archipelagos, Madeira and Azores.

THE NORTH

The North comprises the Minho, Douro and Trás-os-Montes provinces. Minho, the Alto (upper) and Minho proper, and Douro are green and

PORTUGUESE FOOD

vibrant; their coastline is actually known as the 'green coast' (**Costa Verde**). The vines from which the **vinho verde** ('green wine') is made are grown here. The wine is not actually green in colour, of course, but is made with slightly unripe grapes. It is less alcoholic than other wines, very refreshing and has a pleasant sparkle. The vines are grown high above the ground, trained over trees or pergolas, thus saving the space underneath for other crops, although this makes harvesting very difficult. The rivers in this region are rich in salmon, trout and lamprey, all of them used in typical dishes, such as **arroz de lampreia** (lamprey rice).

It was here that the Portuguese nation was born, and as a result the region is known as the 'cradle of Portugal'. Guimarães, in its centre, was the birthplace of the first Portuguese king, Afonso Henriques.

The Minho and Douro provinces are home to many dishes that have become national specialities, like the ubiquitous **caldo verde** (green broth, a favourite soup simply made with a kind of kale cabbage and potatoes, and flavoured with a little **chouriço**), **rojões** (a pork dish), **pastéis de bacalhau** (salt cod cakes), **bacalhau à Gomes de Sá** (salt cod Gomes de Sá fashion), **broa** (a delicious maize bread), **tripas à moda do Porto** (Oporto-style tripe and bean stew) and many delicious desserts, such as **sopa dourada** (a golden soup with egg yolks) and **torta de Viana** (a sponge roll filled with a rich egg sweet). A simple but delicious dessert or snack is **fatias douradas** (golden slices) consisting of slices of bread dipped in egg, fried and covered with sugar and cinnamon (Portugal's favourite spice).

Contrasting with the lushness of the Minhos and Douro provinces, Trás-os-Montes (literally 'beyond the mountains') is austere and sparsely populated. However, the areas are all linked by the famous Douro river, which is very important to the port wine industry, both as a source of water and as a means of transport for the wine, which is taken in barrels by the **rabelo** boats (an ancient type of boat only seen on this river) up to Oporto and Vila Nova de Gaia, opposite, where the port lodges are mainly situated. It is possible, and certainly worthwhile, to visit some of these lodges and taste the wines in their various stages of maturation. Look out for names like **Taylors**, **Sandeman**, **Ferreira**, **Fonseca**, **Croft**, **Calem**, and many others. The grapes themselves are grown more or

PORTUGUESE FOOD

less along the Douro river, in almost inaccessible terraced banks and in relatively poor soil. Only a percentage is used for port, the rest being utilised for excellent table wines.

Trás-os-Montes' capital is Bragança, an ancient city with lovely buildings and a gastronomic tradition which encapsulates all the specialities of the province. Winters are cold in the mountains, so food needs to be warming. Look out for **feijoada** (the local bean stew, enriched with various cuts of pork, both fresh and cured), **posta à mirandesa** (a veal dish from Miranda), **rojões** (a pork dish which is a variation on the one cooked in Minho), **vitela no espeto** (veal cooked on the spit) and **cozido à portuguesa** (a simple, very satisfying dish consisting of various meats and garlic sausage cooked with a variety of vegetables). This dish is a national speciality. The terrain here makes it more difficult to cultivate crops, so the land is mainly used for raising sheep, goats, pigs and some cattle – hence the veal dishes. This province is famous for its many kinds of pork sausages, like **morcela** (made with blood and spices, a delicious sausage for frying and grilling). **Presunto** (cured ham) from Lamego is considered the best. Fish from the rivers is also used widely. The fish is mainly trout, often served cold in an **escabeche** (a special sauce containing vinegar). **Castanhas** (chestnuts) prevail here and are used both fresh and dried in some dishes, including soups. Wild **cogumelos** (mushrooms) are popular as well. A good cheese is **Monte**, made with ewes' milk. **Amêndoas** (almonds), **nozes** (walnuts), **azeitonas** (olives) and **azeite** (olive oil) are common too.

THE CENTRAL REGION

The Central Region comprises the Beiras (three provinces, one with a long coastline and the other two inland), Ribatejo (meaning above the Tagus), which is also inland, and Estremadura, a narrow province on the coast, covering the Lisbon area and the Setúbal peninsula.

The three Beiras are very rich gastronomically, as is the whole region. Beira Alta and Beira Baixa (Upper and Lower Beira), inland, are quite mountainous and one of the great sources of lamb and goat meat. The area of Serra da Estrela (Star Mountain), in Beira Baixa, produces a creamy cheese made from ewes' milk, and considered one of the best cheeses in the world. It is simply called **Serra** (mountain) and has two stages of maturation. The first, after the first cure, when it is wrapped in muslin to keep its shape. This wrapping gives the cheese its characteristic appearance. While creamy like this, it is often eaten with a spoon and tastes delicious. If left for some months it will become dry, but not hard, and then has a completely different but still delicious taste.

These two Beiras are very traditional and there are many beautiful places offering good food. Viseu, the main city in Beira Alta, is at the heart of the Dão wine region, (the red wine is highly recommended) and is renowned for its delicate **bolos de ovos** (egg sweets). Kid and lamb are also served in wonderful roasts and stews but pork is, as in the whole of Portugal, abundant and used chiefly for derivatives – hams and many kinds of **chouriço**. A substantial soup is **rancho** (this name is also given to soldiers' meals and implies a large platter full of a mixture of things, in this case meats, chick-peas, potatoes and other vegetables and pasta). Local **açordas** (bread dishes) are famous, especially **migas à lagareiro** (made with bread, cabbage, salt cod and plenty of olive oil). This dish is traditionally cooked during the making of the oil, as it is coming out of the press. Lamprey, shad and trout are prepared here as well, again using olive oil, spices and herbs, particularly bay leaf and nutmeg. A famous salt-cod dish is **bacalhau assado com batatas a murro** (charcoal-grilled cod with potatoes baked in their skins and then given a 'hammering' using the fist, enabling the potatoes to absorb more of the olive oil surrounding them in the baking tray). Corn is grown here and so the menu includes '**papas**' (a kind of polenta soup). Corn flour is also used to thicken vegetable soups. Rice is another favourite, and **arroz de pato** (duck with rice) is well known. In the mountains game such as wild rabbit and partridge can be found. As in Trás-os-Montes, the Beiras offer veal and beef dishes in addition to other meats. Sweets can be on the heavy side, such as **arroz doce** (rice pudding, which is made on top of the stove), **papas de milho doces** (sweet polenta), **pudim de pão** (bread pudding) and **pudim de requeijão** (ricotta-type cheese pudding). Various small cakes are made with olive oil instead of other fats. Fried cakes also feature, especially at Christmas.

PORTUGUESE FOOD

The third Beira, Beira Litoral, enjoys a sandy coast and rich land, combining the best of both worlds. The Bairrada area, north of Coimbra (the main city) is known for its red and white wines, and for **leitão assado à moda Bairrada** (suckling pig roasted until its skin turns golden brown). This dish has been adopted nationally, but Bairrada's version is still the best. Another main city, Aveiro, in the north of this province, is home to the most wonderful egg sweets, the so-called **ovos moles** (soft eggs), sold in little wooden barrels painted with regional motifs. **Ovos moles** are eaten as a sweet by the spoonful but are normally incorporated into other sweets, as a pouring sauce for puddings and as a delectable filling. Aveiro is also known for splendid **caldeiradas de enguias** (eel stews). Its many canals earn it the nickname of 'the Portuguese Venice'. Beira Litoral's soups are often based on bread and are actually like thick stews. For example, **sopa seca** (dry soup) is made with ham, **chouriço** and other pork meats, beef, cabbage and bread, in layers. This dish is often prepared at Christmas. Eels are popular across the province, and appear frequently on menus, as does salt cod. Try **bacalhau assado com broa** (baked salt cod with a thick layer of crumbled maize bread on top). Lamprey is common here too, generally cooked in a rich stew of wine and accompanied by rice. Apart from charcoal-grilled sardines, Beira Alta also offers various versions of **sardinhas na telha** (sardines cooked on a concave roof tile with plenty of olive oil and seasoning, baked in the oven). There are many delicious dishes made with suckling pig, either roasted or stewed with its own offal. Pork haggis is also common, under the name of **bucho**, with rich fillings of meats and seasonings. Try **pé de porco com feijão** (pigs' trotters with beans). Kid, mutton and lamb are used in the famous local **chanfanas** (rich stews) which are highly seasoned and cooked for a long time to produce an extremely tender and succulent dish. This is a traditional dish served at weddings and other celebrations in the province. The sweets are once again based on eggs and there are some local versions of **arroz doce** (rice pudding). But do try **barriga de freira** (nun's belly), a sweet made with yolks and sugar, which is slightly caramelised and a true delight. Another typical dessert is egg lamprey (**lampreia de ovos**) generally not attempted at home because of the complicated recipe. It consists, once again, of eggs and

PORTUGUESE FOOD

sugar and some ground almonds. You can also find various **pão-de-ló**, a light sponge cake, such as the **pão-de-ló Ovar** (from the town of Ovar) and delicious pastries, like **pastéis de Santa Clara**, filled with ground almonds, egg yolks and sugar, and **pastéis de Tentugal** (Tentugal's pastries) which look like little parcels with an egg filling. Try also **arrufadas de Coimbra**, a kind of sweet bun.

The Ribatejo is an inland province where bulls and horses are raised for bullfights. It is a colourful land of great food. Ribatejo, divided in two by the river Tagus, suffers floods every year which enriches the pasture land. Its capital, the old Santarém, is full of history and is an important gastronomic centre where the yearly food fair, **Festival Nacional de Gastronomia**, is held generally at the end of October. This is a very charismatic province, with Vila Franca de Xira at its centre, a little town where the bulls are let loose on the streets before the bullfighting season, as they do in Pamplona in Spain. Almeirim is known for its melons and for **sopa de pedra** (stone soup) which, despite its name, is a rich soup full of meats, beans and vegetables. The name derives from a local legend involving a beggar monk. Black-eyed beans are used in various soups, as well, such as **sopa de feijão frade com couves** (black-eyed beans and cabbage soup). **Sopa dos campinos** is a salt cod and tomato stew-like soup. There are various dishes made with bread such as **açorda de sável** (shad açorda) and **migas de pão de milho** (made with maize bread, olive oil and garlic). A local custom is to prepare slices of freshly baked bread (wheat or maize) and sprinkle them with a little coarse sea salt and olive oil. These can be eaten with charcoal-grilled sardines or by themselves, for breakfast, and are called **tibornas**. Fish from the river is used in stews. **Fataça** (a kind of mullet) can be cooked inside a concave roof tile, covering the fish with bacon fat and baking it in the oven, covered with another roof tile. A favourite meat is kid. Try **cabrito assado** (roast kid, with a spiced wine marinade) and **cabrito frito** (fried kid, another highly recommended dish). Pork is, of course, on the menu as well – **chispe com feijão** (trotters, beans, cured meats and vegetables) being one of the local dishes, as well as **fígado de porco de cebolada** (pork liver with onions). Desserts are varied and rich in this province. **Fatias de Tomar** (Tomar slices), are a typical dish of this lovely medieval town and consist of slices of sponge made only with egg yolks and served in a light syrup. **Manjar celeste** (celestial food) is another sweet made with eggs, fresh bread crumbs, almonds and sugar. **Palha de Abrantes** (Abrantes straw) is another sweet with eggs. In Tomar the small local cheeses are used to make a pudding called **pudim de queijo**. **Tigeladas de Abrantes** (Abrantes cupfuls) are individually baked custards cooked in special earthenware containers.

Some cakes include olive oil, e.g. **bolo de mel** (honey cake) and **broas podres de Natal** (literally 'rotten little Christmas cakes'). There is a variety of fried cakes made during the Christmas season. The Ribatejo province also produces many excellent red wines.

Estremadura is the most forward-thinking and densely populated province. Lisbon is situated here. The area is prosperous, with wonderful countryside and lovely towns like Alcobaça, Óbidos, Sintra and, further south, Setúbal. Many wines are produced here, and have been known for centuries, such as **Bucelas** and **Colares**. Try the exquisite reds of **Torres Vedras**. Around Setúbal the Muscat wine is a speciality (**vinho Moscatel**). The coastline of this province offers a lot of fish dishes, including the usual **caldeiradas** (fish stews) and grilled sardines, which are fresh and delicious.

The cuisine of this region is more sophisticated than the rest of Portugal and has created a series of starters (now adopted everywhere) in addition to soups. Examples include, **rissóis** (prawn or fish rissoles), **caracóis** (snails), **pataniscas de bacalhau** (salt cod fritters, delicious hot or cold), and salads like **salada de feijão frade** (black-eyed beans with onion, boiled egg, parsley and olive oil). The soups can be based on fish (very much like a fish stew but not as thick and perhaps with some stale bread added) and shellfish. **Sopa de camarão** (prawn soup) is a speciality. **Canja** (a plain but excellent chicken soup) is often on the menu. The famous **caldeiradas** or fish stews can vary from place to place according to the fish used and the amount of seasoning. All are worth trying. **Ameijoas à Bulhão Pato** (clams Bulhão Pato style) are a must, prepared with garlic, olive oil, lemon and the beloved fresh coriander. Crab and lobster are excellent, ask for them by name –

PORTUGUESE FOOD

santola and **lagosta**. **Marisqueiras** (restaurants or bars specialising solely in shellfish) have the widest possible choice of prawns of all sizes and other items. Salt cod is very popular, and **bacalhau à Brás** (cod cooked Brás-style, with thinly fried potatoes, onions and eggs) should not be missed. One of the most popular fish in Portugal is hake, which is served with potatoes and greens, or **filetes de pescada** (hake filleted and fried in batter, generally accompanied by a mixed salad and rice with tomatoes, a very Portuguese side dish). **Peixe espada** (scabbard fish, a long flat narrow fish without scales), which can be silvery or black in colour according to the depth of the waters where it was caught, is hugely popular and delicious fried or grilled. In Portugal you will find many kinds of fish within the **garoupa** (grouper) species, as well as within the sea bass and sea bream families like **cherne**, **robalo**, **pargo** and many others, all excellent poached, fried, grilled or even baked. When in Setúbal **salmonete grelhado** (grilled mullet) must be tried. Among bread dishes, the best in this region is the **açorda de marisco** (seafood **açorda**) a speciality in many Lisbon restaurants. Steaks are considered excellent 'fast food', especially when served as a filling for a sandwich roll, when it is given the name **prego**. A regular steak is **bife**, and if you want it with all the trimmings it is **bife à café**, served with an egg on top and always with chips. A **costeleta de porco grelhada** (grilled pork chop) is equally popular. A Lisbon speciality is **iscas com elas**, a liver dish well seasoned with a marinade and served with boiled potatoes. Two Trás-os-Montes specialities are popular in Lisbon as well – **cozido à portuguesa** (Portuguese-style boiled meats and vegetables) and **feijoada** (meat and bean stew). **Frango de churrasco** (barbecued chicken) is a popular and reasonably priced take-away meal. This must be accompanied by the very finely cut and delicious crisps sold at take-away establishments. Broad beans are eaten all over the country and **favada à portuguesa** (Portuguese broad beans) must be tried. This dish consists of tender broad beans cooked with a variety of smoked meats, onions and fresh coriander.

For pudding, **arroz doce** (rice pudding) as well as **mousse de chocolate** (chocolate mousse) are generally on offer. **Farófias** (floating islands, made with egg whites and custard sauce), **pudim flan** (crème caramel) and **torta de laranja** (orange roll) are also popular. The province has countless cake specialities, such as **pastéis de nata** from Belém in Lisbon (egg custard tarts), **pastéis de feijão** (bean, egg and almond tarts, a speciality from Torres Vedras), **nozes de Cascais** (caramelised walnuts, from Cascais), **queijadas de Sintra** (little cheese cakes) and many others.

Around Lisbon and Setúbal there are many wonderful small cheeses made from ewes' and goats' milk. They may be sold fresh or dried, and are often served as a pre-starter to your meal. They are known as **saloio**. Other famous cheeses from the region are the **Alverca** and the **Azeitão**.

THE SOUTH

The Southern region embraces the Alto and the Baixo Alentejo provinces (Upper and Lower Alentejo) and the Algarve. The two Alentejos are vast, with large estates that cultivate wheat, rice (in some areas near the rivers), olive trees, vines and great expanses of cork-oak trees. Portugal is the world's largest producer of cork and it all comes from this region. The long coastline provides the ingredients for the usual **caldeiradas** (fish stews) and sardines, grilled straight from the sea, but the Alentejo is extraordinarily rich in pork and lamb. The local **chouriços** (spicy sausages, eaten raw or cooked) are excellent, as is the **presunto** (cured ham). The fresh pork meat is delicious and lean as the animals generally roam free and feed on acorns. From the Alentejo comes the (uncooked) fragrant bread soup called **sopa à alentejana** (Alentejo-style soup), consisting of chunks of wonderful local bread soaked in a mixture of olive oil, garlic and fresh coriander, with poached egg on top. This is a filling lunch dish. Bread is a prominent feature here, as this area grows a lot of wheat and is in fact known as the Portuguese 'bread basket'. There are various other soups which use bread as a main ingredient, such as **gaspacho** (varying from the Spanish soup of the same name as this version has finely cut, rather than grated, vegetables which gives the soup a more crunchy texture), **sopa de espinafres com ovos** (spinach and eggs) and **sopa de poejos** (pennyroyal soup, with eggs), among many others. Other popular

PORTUGUESE FOOD

bread dishes are **migas** (where the bread is cooked forming a kind of omelette) which taste delicious. Try **migas à alentejana** (bread with lots of pork meats and garlic). **Borrego** (young lamb) is used in delicate stews and roasts, marinated in the splendid local wine. **Cabrito** (kid) is also common, and interchangeable with lamb in the recipes. Try roast kid (**cabrito assado**) highly seasoned with sweet paprika (**colorau**), wine, garlic and onions. Fats used may be olive oil or lard, or a mixture of both. **Ensopado de borrego** (lamb soaked in bread) is a very rich stew made with lots of onions and other seasonings, and is served on slices of stale bread, instead of potatoes or rice. The bread soaks up the gravy and is delicious. Although pennyroyal is used freely in the Alentejo (but not in other regions of Portugal) the most popular herb is fresh coriander, the national passion. It goes in many dishes (and salads), such as **pezinhos de porco de coentrada** (pork trotters with coriander) and **fígado de coentrada** (pork liver with coriander). **Lombo de porco com amêijoas** (pork fillet with clams) has become a classic, loved all over the country. It is an interesting and successful combination, with the pork cooked with lots of seasonings and the clams added later. The area is also rich in poultry and game (chicken, rabbit, hare, partridge, turkey and woodcock). These are oven roasted (**assado no forno**), normally covered with a layer of bacon fat or in the pot, with wine and spices – i.e. **perdiz à Montemor** (Montemor-fashion partridge, in the oven) and **galinholas à Alentejana** (Alentejo woodcock) cooked with plenty of wine, garlic and other seasonings and a tasty filling. '**Vinha d'alhos**' on the menu means the meat has been marinated in wine and garlic. Chicken pies are a speciality in the Alentejo, mainly in the capital, Évora. They are generally made with puff-pastry and the filling is rich and wonderful. They are equally good hot or cold and many snack-bars and pâtisseries sell them all over the country. Look out for **empadas de galinha** (chicken pies).

Sweets follow the Portuguese tradition using lots of eggs and there are local versions of **arroz doce** (rice pudding), nun's belly (**barriga de freira**) and **toucinho do céu** (bacon from heaven – which is found under various guises in many other provinces). All are made either with yolks and sugar or ground almonds and eggs. Cinnamon is used in many of these puddings. **Sericaia** is a kind of baked custard, drier but very rich and delicious, with plenty of cinnamon. The Alentejo is famous for **boleimas** (cakes made with a sweet-dough base), enriched with olive oil, sugar, eggs and spices. Other cakes made with olive oil are the 'rotten cakes' (**bolos podres**) so-called because of their dark appearance. They are excellent, with lots of honey and cinnamon mixed in the dough. The many convents that existed and still exist here have produced many sweet specialities, delicate small egg cakes, sometimes in the form of little half-moons, called **azevias**. Cheese tarts are also extremely good and popular. Do try **queijadas de requeijão** (ricotta-type cheese tarts) and **queijadas de Évora**, made with ewes' milk fresh cheese. Here, too, there are many fried cakes for the Christmas season. The Estremoz and Elvas areas are known for their marvellous greengages, many of which are preserved and sold world-wide as Elvas plums (**ameixas de Elvas**). The Alentejo has become one of the best sources of extraordinarily good wines in Portugal, especially reds, mainly from the areas of Borba, Redondo and Reguengos. There are various wonderful small cheeses in the Alentejo, normally made with ewes' milk. **Serpa**, **Évora** and **Nisa** are the most outstanding.

THE ALGARVE

The Algarve is, in a way, a world in itself. It enjoys a warm climate even in winter, which makes it suitable for growing, for example, luscious figs, almonds, strawberries and tomatoes. The remaining land is taken up by the long coast, a source of all kinds of seafood in a great variety of dishes. The soups are nearly all made with fish or shellfish – e.g. **sopa de cabeça de peixe** (fish head soup, using the head of a large fish, tomatoes, potatoes, stale bread and seasonings). Starters include **choquinhos com tinta** (squid in its ink) and **amêijoas na cataplana** (clams cooked in a cataplana vessel – a kind of double wok). The **caldeiradas** (fish stews) are particularly good. Tuna is used for canning, but a lot of it is eaten fresh, as well, e.g. **bifes de atum** (tuna steaks) cooked with lots of onion and tomatoes. A speciality to try is **lulas recheadas**, also called **lulas cheias** locally, (small squid stuffed with rice and seasonings), shellfish rice (**arroz de marisco**) and octopus rice

PORTUGUESE FOOD

(**arroz de polvo**). Meats include chicken in various guises and the odd dish with partridge. The best meat dish in the Algarve is the local version of the Alentejo 'pork with clams'. With so many almond trees, the Algarve specialises in almond pastries and little cakes, marzipan-like figures (filled with egg sweet – absolutely delicious) and fig concoctions. Try **queijinhos de amêndoa** (little almond cheeses – on account of the shape), **morgado de figo** (dried figs, with lots of spices, pressed into a round shape) and **figos cheios** (dried figs stuffed with almonds). **Bolos de D. Rodrigo** (D. Rodrigo cakes) are heavenly, made with egg yolks, sugar, almonds and cinnamon, and sold in little pointed foil parcels (to keep the syrup inside).

MADEIRA

The Madeira Archipelago comprises two islands, Madeira itself and Porto Santo. The latter is small, flat and very sandy, depending for its supplies on the larger island and following the same gastronomic traditions.

Madeira is famous the world over mainly because of its unique wine and temperate climate, where tropical and semi-tropical produce are grown, like bananas, passion fruit, paw-paws, mangoes, avocados, and many other fruits, including oranges, apples and so on. Vegetables are also abundant and varied – sweet potato being the local speciality – as well as corn; both are used in many dishes. The island is very mountainous and the land given to agriculture is precious, carefully cultivated in terraces. Every inch is used to advantage, to grow food, vines and tropical flowers.

The fishing industry is one of the main resources here, with big fish like tuna being used fresh in delicious dishes, such as **atum assado**, which is braised tuna with onions and tomatoes. **Bifes de atum** (tuna steaks) are marinated steaks fried and then cooked in the sauce, with herbs, olive oil and tomato. They may be accompanied by potatoes or **milho frito** (polenta fried in cubes). A famous tuna dish for festivities is **atum salpresado**, meaning that the tuna is pressed with salt for a couple of days. It is then cooked with red beans and served with sweet potatoes, corn and salad. Another very common fish in Madeira is the scabbard fish and because the waters around the island are very deep, the fish

PORTUGUESE FOOD

has black skin instead of silvery. Scabbard fish is called **espada** (sword) in Madeira on account of its very long and smooth body. The humble **cavala** (mackerel) is also a popular fish. Try **cavalas com molho de vilão** (mackerel with villain sauce), which means that the fish is marinated and then fried, served with a sauce prepared with the reduced marinade. Despite the abundance of fish, salt cod is also popular in Madeira, as elsewhere in Portugal. Soups in Madeira are heavy and meant as a meal in themselves – like **sopa de moganga**, a local soup made with pumpkin. Apart from the pumpkin it contains plenty of beef, pasta and various vegetables. One of Madeira's specialities is the very Portuguese **cozido**, in this case called **cozido à Madeirense** (boiled meats and vegetables Madeira style), perhaps because the meat used here is pork, instead of beef. It also contains pumpkin and couscous (another difference). Marinated pork is also used for **carne de vinha d'alhos** (the meat is marinated for two to three days and cooked until tender). It is then fried in pork fat together with bread and various accompaniments, like sweet potato and new potatoes. This dish is the most celebrated meat dish in Madeira and is eaten during the Christmas festivities. Other dishes served on special occasions, including Christmas, are **carne assada**, (roast beef or pork) and **sarapatel**, which is made with pork blood and liver (during the 'slaughter season').

Another typical dish is **espetada**, chunks of beef on a very large sort of kebab which is shared among the people at the table. A common accompaniment for various dishes is **milho frito**, squares of fried polenta (made from maize flour). For dessert there are cakes and puddings made with **mel de cana** (molasses) – sugar cane is cultivated here – and one of the best is **bolo de mel da Madeira** (Madeira honey cake), a dark delight with lots of spices, traditionally eaten during Christmas but sold all year round. Sweet potato is another local ingredient for cakes, e.g. **fartes de batata** (squares of sweet potato purée with spices and almonds). **Queijadas da Madeira** (Madeira small cheese cakes) are another speciality. All sweets will of course be served with that other local treasure, **Madeira wine**, one of the finest in the world.

PORTUGUESE FOOD

THE AZORES

The Azores are situated in the middle of the Atlantic, between Europe and America. Many weather systems develop around this area, resulting in a wet climate. This makes the islands green and luxuriant, with good pasture-land and good cattle, hence the very famous local **queijo da Ilha**, 'island's cheese', meaning **queijo de S. Jorge** – S. Jorge's island cheese. It is a cheddar-style cheese, but more piquant and less dense. Most islands produce their own cheese however, and although of the same kind, they can vary in strength and texture. Generally they are all very good. Pineapples are another very important product, grown in immense nurseries with the temperature carefully controlled. The quality is excellent.

The nine islands forming this archipelago are, according to legend, what is left of the lost continent of Atlantis. Most are beautiful and some have old craters now full of water, forming lovely lakes. The place is known for its wild blue hydrangeas, lush vegetation and temperate climate (despite the rain). There are mineral water springs here and, curiously, geysers. In the island of S. Miguel the Furnas lagoon has numerous small volcanic craters, locally called **caldeiras**, where the Azorians cook their famous **cozido** (meats and vegetables) for five hours, in a big pot which is lowered into one of the natural holes.

Various local soups include a little vinegar and because of this are called **azedas** (sour), such as **sopa azeda de feijão** (a bean soup, with vegetables and bread, sweet potatoes and cinnamon as well as a spoonful of vinegar). Each island offers its own version or versions not only of this soup but also of **sopa do Espírito Santo** (Holy Spirit soup) made with lots of meats, vegetables, bread, herbs and spices. This is served during religious festivals. **Sopa de funcho** (fennel soup with beans and bacon fat) is another favourite.

Seafood is of course abundant. Try **lapas Afonso** (limpets served with a tasty onion sauce) as a starter. Limpets are also used with rice (**arroz de lapas**) and stewed octopus is popular (**polvo guisado**). Mackerel and grouper are abundant and are stuffed and baked (**cavala** and **garoupa recheada**). The locals appreciate meat rather than fish, though, and have good beef and pork. A speciality is **carne de vaca à antiga** (beef old-fashioned style), which is seasoned in a rich marinade, then roasted to perfection and served with new potatoes. One of the island's crops is **inhame** (yam) which is used a lot as a side dish instead of pasta or rice. If in the Azores, try their favourite dessert, **pudim de coalhada** (a kind of fresh cheese pudding, rich and delicious). There are many local cakes of all sizes. A fruit cake for Christmas is simply called **bolo de Natal**, but do try also **fofas do Faial** (Faial's soft cakes), **covilhetes de leite** (custard tarts), **pastéis de arroz** (rice tarts) and **esperanças** (delicate little cakes filled with almonds).

There is a good local wine (**verdelho**) which in times past used to be exported and greatly appreciated by Russian Tsars. There are also various good local liqueurs, like **tangerina** (mandarin) and **leite** (milk).

A local speciality is moulded sugar made into a variety of shapes. This is called **alfenim** and is an art in itself.

FESTIVE FOOD

As a Catholic country, Portugal celebrates lots of Saint days and other important dates from the religious calendar.

Christmas is obviously the most prominent of these celebrations and the traditional supper on the 24th, after Midnight Mass, is **bacalhau com todos** (poached salt cod with potatoes and vegetables), laced with olive oil, followed by a great variety of cakes, including fried ones (**filhoses**) which are sprinkled with sugar and cinnamon or dipped into honey or syrup.

In the Minho province, where the tradition of eating salt cod for this special supper originated, there may also be **polvo com arroz** (octopus with rice) and **pastéis de bacalhau** (salt cod cakes), on this occasion.

Lunch on the 25th is a large and lengthy meal, starting perhaps with the salt cod left-overs – if there were any – reheated in olive oil and garlic or **canja** (chicken soup) and stuffed turkey or capon, with a long list of desserts, such as creamy rice-pudding (**arroz doce**) – which in Portugal is made on top of the stove and is very special, **sopa dourada**

PORTUGUESE FOOD

a dessert made with sponge cake, yolks of eggs, sugar and cinnamon, fruit salad (**salada de fruta**) laced with port or madeira wine, nuts and dried fruits.

In Madeira pork is served as **carne de vinha d'alhos** (pork fillet in a strong marinade of wine and garlic), **carne assada** (roast leg of pork) and **sarapatel** (a dish made with pig's blood and liver, dried fruits and lots of seasonings). These are the real Christmas treats, followed by the dark and deliciously spicy **bolo de mel** (molasses cake). The Azores have their own dark cake, **bolo de Natal**, with crystallised fruits, served with **licor de leite** (milk liqueur) or **licor de tangerina** (mandarin liqueur).

Nuts, fruits and cakes (especially the fried ones) will be prepared in large quantities, to last until 'dia de Reis' (6th January, Epiphany), when **Bolo Rei** (the King's cake) is obligatory. This consists of a ring made with a sweet dough with dried and crystallised fruits. Good table wines accompany these meals, which are followed by home-made liqueurs and port or Madeira.

Carnival is celebrated with parades and pork dishes in various provinces (this being pig-slaughter time) and in Trás-os-Montes they also serve **cozido à portuguesa** (Portuguese boiled meats, a tasty mixture of various meats and vegetables) which is a national dish. Generally speaking, there aren't many other specific dishes for Carnival. In the Azores they serve **fofas do Faial** (fluffy cakes from the Faial Island), a kind of choux-pastry filled with cream or custard.

At Easter, sugared almonds (**amêndoas doces**) are sold in vast quantities all over Portugal and given as presents to children. **Folar**, a sweet loaf with spices, is topped with boiled eggs, to symbolise the season.

Although each village and town remembers its own Patron Saint with festivities and good food, the most celebrated saints are the so-called 'popular saints of June', revered all over the country: St. Anthony, St. John and St. Peter (13th, 24th and 29th June). **Cabrito assado** (roast kid) is eaten in the North, while in Lisbon and the South sardines (**sardinhas assadas**) are barbecued out of doors through the warm nights, amid songs and folk dances.

PORTUGUESE FOOD

EATING OUT/MEAL TIMES/EATING PLACES

There is a great choice of places to eat in Portugal and it is easy to find reasonably priced food all over the country. Wherever drinks are sold, there will also be some kind of food. A **bar** serves alcoholic and soft drinks and coffee or tea, perhaps from 8 am to midnight. They have snacks such as meat croquettes and prawn rissoles (**croquetes de carne** and **rissóis de camarão**), steak in a roll (**prego**), steak on a plate with chips and fried egg (**bitoque**), and a few other savoury snacks, as well as some cakes (**bolos**). They may also have light meals. **Cafés** and **Cafetarias** are popular places where one can also get snacks, coffee, tea and soft drinks, and, like pâtisseries (**pastelarias**), they open from 8 or 9 am to 10 or 12 at night, depending on the area. These establishments also serve sandwiches (**sandes**), toasts (**torradas**) and toasted sandwiches (**tostas**), light meals and a great variety of cakes at which the Portuguese excel, a soup (**sopa**), various filled croissants (**croissant recheado**), meat pies and chicken pies (**empadas**), salt cod cakes (**pastéis de bacalhau**) and other savouries. Elegant pâtisseries may be called tea-houses (**casa de chá**), in which case they are more select and a little more expensive.

A **Cervejaria** (beer house) is popular for a meal or snack, with local cold beer of good quality (**cerveja**) served generally with tit-bits like nuts or crisps or the very Portuguese **tremoços** (lupin seeds). Many beer houses have a good selection of seafood and the menus are varied. They are opened from before lunch time until around midnight.

Open-air cafés and restaurants (**esplanadas**) are popular both during the summer and winter, serving anything from a coffee to a full meal.

Restaurants vary greatly in quality, price and variety of dishes served. The only way of knowing is to look at the menus displayed at the door or window, which will list what is available and the cost. If on a budget the **menu turístico** (tourists' menu) is a good bet, including one starter (**entrada**) or soup (**sopa**) and a main dish (**prato principal**) with various choices between meat and fish, plus dessert. It is possible to get a **meia-dose** (half-portion) of some dishes in the general menu and this is

PORTUGUESE FOOD

wise sometimes, given the large amounts served. Most popular restaurants do this. Restaurants open for lunch and dinner (from 12.30 to 3 pm and 7 or 7.30 to 11 pm or so). Those specialising in **frango à piri-piri** (barbecued chicken with chilli) are called **Churrasqueira**. The chicken is terrific but you must ask for **pouco picante** (mild) if you do not want it very hot. You will also find restaurants serving only shellfish (**Marisqueira**) and they will generally have live seafood displayed in the window. But you can have shellfish and seafood in most good restaurants as well. For a cheap but homely meal look for a **casa de pasto**. **Tascas** and **Tasquinhas** are names for small taverna-type eating and drinking places, some cheap and geared to local tradesmen (although the food will be good) and others more trendy.

READING THE MENU

Menus are divided into **Entradas** (starters), which may include the **Sopas** (soups), **Peixe e Marisco** (fish and shellfish), **Carnes** (meats), **Acompanhamentos** (side dishes) – which may include the **Saladas** (salads) – and **Sobremesas** (dessert). **Queijos** (cheeses) may be mentioned separately from the dessert. More homely eating places may simply have a long list of dishes available, whether fish or meat. The menus will also indicate which dishes, if any, can be served in half-portions, in which case they will show both prices. A **meia-dose** (half-portion) is always adequate for one person and certainly for children.

entradas	starters
acepipes	appetizers
sopas	soups
peixe e marisco	fish and shellfish
pratos de carne	meat dishes (always served with chips and rice)
ovos	eggs, generally served with chips
acompanhamentos	side dishes
legumes	vegetables
saladas	salads
sobremesas	desserts (puddings, fruit salads, fruit, ice-cream)
queijos	cheese (a selection)

DRINKS

DRINKS

There are many excellent mineral waters to choose from, either still or sparkling. The local industry is prolific in the production of good canned and bottled fruit juices and drinks. Locally made beers are of a high quality and always served cold (**fresca**). Coffee is generally good and served in a variety of sizes, which you must specify (see below). Tea is normally served plain and weak, unless otherwise stated. Herbal teas (**tisanas**) are also available.

Beer is very popular in Portugal, despite an abundance of excellent local wines. There is a long tradition of beer making and drinking. Lunch is often accompanied by beer and beer houses themselves (**cervejarias**) serve good food. Just as with the coffee, there are specific nicknames for the various sizes of glass: **imperial** is a small glass, the next size up is a **caneca**, and what would be considered a pint is a **girafa**. Beers can also be bottled and canned, white or dark (**branca/preta**). Small dishes of appetisers are often served with beers.

água mineral com gás *sparkling mineral water*
água mineral sem gás *still mineral water*
amarguinha *bitter-almond liqueur made in the Algarve region*
aniz *aniseed liqueur*
aguardente *brandy-type spirit. Can be* **velha** *(old) and* **velhíssima** *(very old). It is very good after a meal served with coffee.*
bagaceira *eau-de-vie-type spirit made with the leftovers of pressed grapes. Strong and fragrant and good with coffee after a heavy meal.*
batido de fruta *milkshake with fruit*
batido de morango *strawberry milkshake*
branco *white*
café *coffee*
  bica *small, strong black coffee (espresso)*
  carioca *small but slightly weaker black coffee*
  galão *large white coffee generally served in a glass*
  garoto *small white coffee*
  meia de leite *ordinary size cup of milky coffee*

DRINKS

carioca de limão *lemon infusion*
cerveja *beer/lager*
chá *tea*
chá com leite *tea with milk*
chá com limão *tea with lemon*
chá forte *strong tea*
chocolate frio *cold chocolate drink*
chocolate quente *hot chocolate*
ginjinha *morello-cherry liqueur typical of Portugal*
granizado de café *cool coffee drink with crushed ice*
laranjada engarrafada *bottled orange juice*
laranjada natural *fresh orange juice*
leite *milk*
leite frio/quente *cold/hot milk*
limonada *lemonade*
sumo de fruta *fruit juice*
  ananás *pineapple*
  laranje *orange*
  maçã *apple*
  pêra *pear*
  pêssego *peach*
  tomate *tomato*
  uva *grape*
tinto *red wine*
tisana de camomila *camomile tea*
tisana de Lúcia-Lima *vervaine tea*
vinho branco *white wine*
vinho tinto *red wine*
vinho verde *'green wine' slightly sparkling white wine*
vinhos espumantes *sparkling wines*
xarope *syrup*
  xarope de groselha *blackcurrant syrup*
  xarope de morango *strawberry syrup*

The most incredible variety of grapes, many unique to the country, grow in most parts of Portugal and even when the wine is not produced commercially, those with a plot of land will make wine for their own consumption. Rosé wine is generally frowned upon in Portugal itself, despite being successfully exported to several countries. Red wines (**tinto**) is actually the best choice and there are now countless labels to choose from. The Douro region, best known for port wine production, is offering some seriously good wines made from the same grapes (given that by law only about half to two thirds of them are allowed to go into port making). Dão wines are already well established. The Bairrada region (around the Coimbra area) produces intriguing wines, as well as the Ribatejo. Estremadura is another prolific region and the Alentejo has become the latest revelation, with many excellent wines. Whites (**branco**) are also produced in all regions but only the Minho province offers the famous **Vinho Verde**, so apt for drinking (very cool) on its own or with light food. It is a good party wine.

At restaurants there will be the **carta dos vinhos** (wine list) with national and international wine. If you are looking for a reasonably-priced wine, the **vinho da casa** (house wine) is normally quite good and inexpensive. You can also get it in half bottles (**meia garrafa**). State whether you want **tinto** (red) or **branco** (white). Bottled wines are subject to rigorous controls in order to maintain quality. There are demarcated regions (**regiões demarcadas**) and the best wines will indicate this with the initials **DOC** (**denominação de origem controlada**) but those with **Vinho Regional** (regional wine) stated on the label are also subject to controls.

vinho verde dry, young wine, slightly sparkling from the Minho region. Must be served chilled as an aperitif or with seafood or light meat dishes.

vinho branco seco dry white wine generally served chilled with seafood

vinho branco meio-seco medium dry white wine served cool

vinho tinto meio-encorpado red, medium-bodied for heavier fish and salt cod dishes or sardines and light meats. From Borba, Dão and Ribatejo regions. Serve at room temperature.

WINES

vinho tinto velho mature red wine for red meats. From the Alentejo, Bairrada, Dão, Douro, Ribatejo and Palmela regions. Serve at room temperature.

vinho tinto encorpado full-bodied red wine for red meats. From the Alentejo, Bairrada, Dão, Douro, Ribatejo and Palmela regions. Serve at room temperature.

moscatel de Setúbal Setúbal's special muscat-grape wine, medium-sweet. A fantastic dessert wine, DOC labelled.

vinhos espumantes Champagne-type wines, from the Bairrada region. These wines come in the typically-shaped champagne bottle and are quite acceptable. They can be sweet (**doce**), medium-sweet (**meio-doce**) or dry (**seco**). Serve very cool.

Vinhos do Porto Port wines, good on their own at any time, as aperitifs and to end a meal, according to their sweetness. The grapes for Port are all grown along the Douro river, which meets the sea at Oporto. Port wines go from dry to quite sweet – check the label. Dry Ports should be served cool (**fresco**), the others at room temperature (**natural**). If in Oporto, try to visit one of the many lodges for tasting.

Vinhos de Madeira Madeira wines are also something unique. Because of the special way that they are matured, Madeira wines last practically forever, even after they are opened. Again they go from dry (**seco**) to sweet (**doce**) and the rules are the same as for port wines. Apart from their exquisite quality for drinking, they are also marvellous for enhancing sauces and fruit salads.

Both Port and Madeira wines are exceedingly good with some foods, apart from desserts, cheese or nuts. For example, game, pâté and duck.

...à caçadora *hunter-style (poultry or game marinated in wine and garlic)*
...à jardineira *garden-style with vegetables like green beans and carrots*
...à lagareiro *baked dish made with lots of olive oil*
...à portuguesa *Portuguese fashion, i.e. with tomato sauce*
abóbora *pumpkin*
açafrão *saffron*
acepipes *appetisers*
acompanhamentos *side dishes*
açorda *typical Portuguese dish with bread*
açorda com peixe frito *thick bread soup accompanying fried fish*
açorda de alho *thick bread soup with garlic and beaten egg (generally served with fried fish in traditional restaurants)*
açorda de marisco *thick bread soup with shellfish and a beaten egg, typical of the Lisbon area*
açorda de sável *thick bread soup with shad*
açúcar *sugar*
água *water*
albardado *in batter*
alcachofras *artichokes*
alcatra *braised beef, typical of the Azores*
aletria *fine noodles*
alface *lettuce*
alheiras *chicken and garlic sausage from Trás-os-Montes*
alho *garlic*
alho francês *leek*
almoço *lunch*
almôndegas *meatballs*
alperces *apricots*
amêijoas *clams*
amêijoas à Bulhão Pato *clams with garlic and coriander*
amêijoas na cataplana *clams cooked in a 'cataplan' pot, with **chouriço** and herbs*
ameixa *plum*
ameixas de Elvas *Elvas plums*
ameixa seca *prune*
amêndoas *almonds*

MENU READER

amendoim *peanut*
amora *blackberry*
ananás *pineapple*
anchovas *anchovies*
areias de Cascais *small cookies from Cascais*
arjamolho *kind of gazpacho soup, typical of the Algarve*
arroz branco *plain rice*
arroz de ervilhas *pea rice*
arroz de frango *chicken with rice*
arroz de lampreia *lamprey with rice*
arroz de marisco *shellfish with rice*
arroz de pato *rice with duck*
arroz de polvo *octopus with rice*
arroz de tomate *tomato rice*
arroz doce *rice pudding Portuguese-style made on top of the stove
with lemon rind, vanilla and topped with cinnamon*
arroz no forno *rice cooked in the oven*
arrufadas de Coimbra *sweet buns*
assado *roasted*
assado no forno *oven-roasted*
assado no espeto *spit roasted*
atum *tuna fish*
atum assado *braised tuna with onions and tomatoes*
atum de conserva *canned tuna*
avelã *hazelnut*
azeite *olive oil*
azeitonas *olives (black or green)*
azevias *half-moon shaped cakes*
bacalhau *salt cod*
bacalhau à Brás *typical delicious dish with salt cod, onion and
potatoes all bound with scrambled eggs*
bacalhau à Gomes de Sá *good salt cod dish with layers of potatoes,
onions and boiled eggs, laced with olive oil and baked*
bacalhau à lagareiro *salt cod baked with lots of olive oil*
bacalhau com natas *salt cod in cream sauce au gratin*
bacalhau com todos *salt cod poached with potatoes and vegetables*

bacalhau assado *charcoal-grilled cod*
bacalhau na brasa *salt cod grilled on charcoal, served with olive oil*
banana *banana*
banha *lard*
barriga de freira *a sweet made with yolks and sugar, slightly caramelised*
batata *potato*
batatas a murro *potatoes baked in their own skin and then soaked in olive oil*
batatas assadas/fritas *baked potatoes/chips*
batatas cozidas *boiled potatoes*
batata doce *sweet potato*
batata doce assada *baked sweet potato*
baunilha *vanilla*
bem passado *well done*
beringela *aubergine*
beterraba *beetroot*
bife *steak (and chips and perhaps fried egg)*
bife à café *steak in cream sauce served with an egg on top (with chips)*
bife do lombo *sirloin steak*
bifes de atum *tuna steaks*
bifes de perú *turkey steaks*
biscoitos *cookies*
biscoitos de azeite *olive oil biscuits*
bitoque *steak with fried egg and chips*
bolachas *biscuits*
bolachas de água e sal *water biscuits (crackers)*
boleimas *cakes with a bread dough base with olive oil, sugar, eggs and spices*
bolo de chocolate *chocolate cake*
bolo de mel *honey cake*
bolo de mel da Madeira *Madeira molasses cake made with lots of spices and eaten traditionally at Christmas*
bolo podre *delicious dark cake made with honey, olive oil and spices*
bolos *cakes*
bolos de D. Rodrigo *cakes made with egg yolks, sugar, almonds and cinnamon, and sold in little pointed foil parcels to keep the syrup inside*

MENU READER

bolos de ovos *egg cakes*
borrego *lamb*
broa *a crusty rustic maize bread*
broas de mel *small honey cakes eaten at Christmas*
broas podres de Natal *small spicy cakes eaten at Christmas*
brócolos *broccoli*
bucho *pork haggis*
cabrito *kid*
cabrito assado *roast kid with a spiced marinade*
cabrito frito *fried kid*
caça *game*
cacau *cocoa*
caldeirada *fish stew*
caldeirada à fragateira *seafood stew*
caldeirada de enguias *eel stew*
caldeirada de peixe *fish stew*
caldo *broth*
caldo verde *green broth, made with shredded kale and potatoes with a little* **chouriço**
camarões *shrimps*
canela *cinnamon*
canja *chicken soup*
capilé *drink made with iced coffee, lemon rind and sugar*
caracóis *snails (small, cooked in a tasty broth and served with a toothpick)*
caranguejo *crab*
carapau *horse mackerel*
caril *curry*
carne *meat*
carne assada *roast meat (generally beef)*
carne de porco à alentejana *highly seasoned pork dish with clams, typical of the Alentejo*
carne de vaca *beef*
carne de vaca assada *roast beef*
carneiro *mutton*
castanha *chestnut*

castanhas assadas *roasted chestnuts*
castanhas cozidas *boiled chestnuts with aniseed*
cavala *mackerel*
cebola *onion*
cenouras *carrots*
cerejas *cherries*
chanfana *rich stew*
chanfana da Bairrada *kid stew*
cherne *species of grouper with dark skin*
chila or **gila** *type of pumpkin (spaghetti squash) made into jam, used as a filling for many cakes and desserts all over Portugal*
chispe com feijão *trotters with beans, cured meats and vegetables*
chocolate *chocolate*
chocos com tinta *cuttlefish in its own ink*
choquinhos *squid*
choquinhos com tinta *squid in its ink*
chouriço *spicy smoked sausage*
churrasco *barbecued/cooked on charcoal*
codorniz *quail*
coelho *rabbit*
coelho à caçadora *hunter's rabbit or hare, cooked in wine and herbs*
coentrada *with coriander*
coentros *fresh coriander*
cogumelos *mushrooms*
colorau *sweet paprika*
compota *jam or compote*
costeletas de porco *pork chops*
couve *cabbage*
couve-flor *cauliflower*
cozido *boiled or poached*
cozido à portuguesa *boiled meats and vegetables*
cravinhos *cloves*
croissants com fiambre *ham-filled croissant*
croissant recheados *filled croissants*
croquettes *meat croquettes*
doce de fruta *jam*

MENU READER

dourada *sea bream*
eirós *large eel generally fried and served with an* **escabeche** *sauce*
empadas *small chicken or veal pies*
enguias de caldeirada *eel stew, typical of Aveiro*
enguias fritas *fried eels*
ensopado *fish or meat stew served on bread slices*
entradas *starters*
entrecosto *entrecôte steak*
erva-doce *aniseed*
ervilhas *peas*
ervilhas com paio e ovos *peas with garlic sausage and poached eggs*
escabeche *a special sauce containing vinegar, normally served with cold fried fish*
espada *name given in Madeira to* **peixe espada** *(scabbard fish)*
espadarte *swordfish*
espadarte fumado *smoked swordfish*
esparguete *spaghetti*
espargos *asparagus*
esparregado *spinach purée with garlic*
especiarias *spices*
espetada *kebab*
espinafres *spinach*
estufado *braised*
farinha *flour*
farófias *'floating islands' made with egg whites and custard sauce*
fataça *grey mullet*
fatias de Tomar *sponge slices served in a light syrup*
fatias douradas *slices of bread dipped in egg, fried and covered with sugar and cinnamon*
favada à portuguesa *broad beans cooked with smoked meats, onions and coriander*
favas *broad beans*
febras *thin slices of roast pork*
feijão *beans*
feijão verde cozido *boiled French beans*
feijoada *bean stew with pork meat and* **chouriço**

MENU READER

fiambre *ham*
fígado *liver*
fígado de porco de cebolada *pork liver with onions*
figos *figs*
figos cheios *dried figs stuffed with almonds*
filetes de pescada *hake fillet in batter*
folhados de carne *meat pastries*
frango *young chicken*
frango à piri-piri *barbecued tender chicken wih chilli*
frango assado *roast tender chicken*
frango no churrasco *barbecued tender chicken in a hot sauce*
frito *fried*
fruta da época *fruit in season*
fumado *smoked*
galinha *chicken*
galinhola *woodcock*
gambas *large prawns*
gambas na chapa *large prawns cooked on the hot plate*
garoupa *grouper*
garoupa recheada *stuffed and baked grouper*
gaspacho *cold soup with finely cut vegetables*
gelado *ice-cream*
grão *chickpeas*
gratinado *au gratin*
grelhado *grilled*
grelhado misto *mixed grill*
guisado *stewed*
inhame *yam, very popular on some of the Azores*
iscas *typical pork liver dish made with wine and garlic*
iscas com elas *well-seasoned liver dish served with boiled potatoes*
jantar *dinner*
lagosta *lobster*
lagostins *king prawns*
lampreia de ovos *egg lamprey, a rich dessert*
lanche *afternoon snack consisting of tea and cakes or buttered toast*
lapas *limpets, popular in Madeira and the Azores*

MENU READER

laranja *orange*
laranja descascada *peeled orange*
lebre *hare*
legumes *vegetables*
leitão à Bairrada *suckling pig crisply roasted*
leite *milk*
leite-creme *crème brûlée*
limão *lemon*
língua *tongue*
língua estufada *braised tongue*
linguado *sole*
linguado frito *fried sole*
linguado grelhado *grilled sole*
lombinho de porco *pork loin*
lombo de porco *pork fillet*
louro *bay leaf*
lulas *squid*
lulas à Algarvia *squid in garlic, Algarve style*
lulas guisadas *stewed squid*
lulas recheadas *small squid stuffed with rice and seasonings*
maçã *apple*
maçã assada *large baked russet apple*
macedónia de frutas *mixed fruit salad*
mal passado *rare*
manga *mango*
manjar celeste *sweet made with eggs, bread crumbs, almonds and sugar*
manteiga *butter*
marisco *shellfish*
marmelada *quince jam – excellent with cheese*
marmelo *quince, a popular fruit, often baked*
massa *pasta*
mel *honey*
mel de cana *molasses*
melancia *watermelon*
melão *melon*

melão com presunto *melon with cured ham slices, a starter*
merenda *afternoon snack consisting of tea and cakes or buttered toast*
merendinha *pastry filled with **chouriço** or **presunto** (ham)*
merengue *meringue*
mexilhões *mussels*
migas *bread cooked with different, well-seasoned ingredients*
migas à alentejana *thick bread soup with pork meat and garlic*
migas à lagareiro *bread cooked with cabbage, salt cod and olive oil*
migas de pão de milho *thick maize bread soup with olive oil and garlic*
milho *corn (maize)*
milho frito *polenta fried in cubes*
miolos *brains*
molho *sauce*
molho béchamel *béchamel sauce*
molho de caril *curry sauce*
molho de escabeche *a special sauce containing vinegar, normally served with cold fried fish*
molho de tomate *tomato sauce*
Monte *cheese made with ewes' milk*
morangos *strawberries*
morcela *pork sausage made with blood and spices*
morgado de figo *dried pressed figs with spices*
mousse de chocolate *chocolate mousse*
...na brasa *on charcoal*
...na frigideira *cooked in the pan (steak - **bife**)*
nabo *turnip*
natas *cream*
...no espeto *kebab*
...no forno *roasted or cooked in the oven*
nozes *walnuts*
omeleta de cogumelos *mushroom omelette*
omeleta de fiambre *ham omelette*
omeleta de queijo *cheese omelette*
omeleta simples *plain omelette*
ostras *oysters*
ovos *eggs*

MENU READER

ovos cozidos *boiled eggs*
ovos escalfados *poached eggs*
ovos estrelados *fried eggs*
ovos mexidos *scrambled eggs*
ovos moles *soft egg sweet*
paio *thick smoked sausage made with lean meat*
palha de Abrantes *sweet made with eggs, looking like straw*
panados *slices of meat coated in egg and breadcrumbs and fried*
pão *bread*
pão de centeio *rye bread*
pão de forma *sliced bread for toast*
pão-de-ló *light sponge cake*
pão de milho *maize bread*
pão saloio *peasant loaf*
papas *polenta soup*
papas de milho doces *sweet polenta*
papo seco *bread roll*
pargo *red bream*
parrilhada *grilled fish*
passas de uva *raisins*
pastéis de bacalhau *salt cod cakes*
pastéis de feijão *tarts made with beans, eggs and almonds*
pastéis de nata *egg custard tarts*
pastéis de Santa Clara *pastries with a filling of almonds, egg yolk and sugar*
pastéis de Tentugal *small pastries with an egg filling*
pataniscas (de bacalhau) *salt cod fritters*
paté de figado *liver pâté*
pato *duck*
pato assado com arroz *roast duck with rice*
pé de porco com feijão *pigs' trotters with beans*
peixe *fish*
peixe assado/cozido/frito/grelhado *baked/poached/fried/grilled fish*
peixe e marisco *fish and shellfish*
peixe-espada *scabbard fish*
peixe espada frito *fried scabbard fish*

MENU READER

peixe espada grelhado *grilled scabbard fish*
peixinhos da horta *French beans fried in batter*
pepino *cucumber*
pequeno almoço *breakfast*
pêra *pear*
percebes *barnacles, highly prized shellfish*
perdiz *partridge*
perdiz com couve lombarda *partridge with cabbage*
perú *turkey*
pescada *hake*
pescada com todos *hake poached with potatoes and vegetables*
pêssego *peach*
pêssego careca *nectarine*
pezinhos de porco de coentrada *pork trotters with coriander and garlic*
pimenta *pepper*
pimentos *peppers*
pimentos assados *grilled peppers*
pinhoada *bar made with pressed pinenuts and caramelised sugar*
pinhões *peanuts*
polvo *octopus*
polvo grelhado *grilled octopus*
polvo guisado *stewed octopus*
pombo *pigeon*
porco *pork*
porco à alentejana *traditional dish with pork, clams and herbs*
porco assado *roast pork*
posta à mirandesa *veal Miranda-style*
prato principal *main dish*
pratos de carne *meat dishes*
pregado *turbot*
prego *steak in a roll*
prego no prato *steak with fried egg and chips*
presunto *cured ham*
pudim da casa *restaurant's own dessert (often a type of crème caramel)*
pudim de pão *bread pudding*
pudim de queijo *cheese pudding*

MENU READER

pudim de requeijão *ricotta-type cheese pudding*
pudim flan *crème caramel*
pudim Molotov *egg-white pudding with egg sauce or caramel*
puré de batata *mashed potato*
queijadas de Évora *cheese tarts made with cheese from ewes' milk*
queijadas de requeijão *ricotta-type cheese tarts*
queijadas de Sintra *little cheese cakes*
queijinhos frescos *small fresh cheeses (ewes' milk, generally)*
queijinhos secos *small dried cheeses*
queijo *cheese*
queijo da Ilha *cheddar-type cheese from the Azores*
queijo da Serra *buttery cheese from Estrela Mountain, a soft, runny cheese made with ewes' milk*
queijo de cabra *goats' cheese*
queijo de ovelha *small, dried ewes' milk cheeses*
queijo fresco *fresh cheese (generally small)*
queijo saloio *small cheese made with ewes' milk or a mixture of goats' and ewes' milk*
raia *skate*
rancho *a substantial soup*
recheado com *stuffed/filled with...*
requeijão *fresh curd cheese resembling ricotta*
rim (rins) *kidney*
rins à Madeira *kidneys served in Madeira wine sauce*
rins com vinho do Porto *kidneys in port wine sauce*
rissóis de camarão/peixe *shrimp or fish rissoles*
robalo *sea bass*
rojões *crisp pieces of marinated pork*
sal *salt*
salada *salad*
salada de feijão frade *black-eyed bean salad, with boiled egg olive oil and seasonings*
salada de fruta *fruit salad*
salada de polvo *a starter with cold octopus, seasoned with olive oil, coriander, onion and vinegar*
salada mista *mixed salad (tomato, lettuce, cucumber, onion)*

MENU READER

salada russa *Russian salad*
salgados *savouries (snacks)*
salmão *salmon*
salmonetes grelhados *grilled red mullet in a butter and lemon sauce*
salpicão *slices of large* **chouriço**
salsa *parsley*
salsichas *sausages*
salteado *sautéed*
sandes *sandwich*
sandes de fiambre *cooked ham sandwich*
sandes de lombo *steak sandwich*
sandes de presunto *cured ham sandwich*
sandes de queijo *cheese sandwich*
santola *spider crab*
sapateira *crab (generally dressed)*
sardinhas assadas *charcoal-grilled sardines*
sardinhas na telha *sardines cooked on a roof tile with olive oil and seasoning, baked in the oven*
sável *shad*
sericaia *baked custard with cinnamon*
sobremesas *desserts*
solha *plaice*
sopa *soup*
sopa à alentejana *soup Alentejo-style, made with chunks of bread, olive oil, fresh coriander and garlic, topped with poached egg*
sopa azeda de feijão *bean soup with vegetables and bread, sweet potatoes cinnamon and a spoonful of vinegar*
sopa de cabeça de peixe *fish head soup, using the head of a large fish, tomatoes, potatoes, stale bread and seasonings*
sopa de camarão *prawn soup*
sopa de castanhas piladas *hearty soup made with chestnuts, beans and rice*
sopa de ervilhas *pea soup*
sopa de espinafres *spinach soup*
sopa de feijão *bean soup with vegetables*
sopa de feijão frade *soup with black-eyed beans*

MENU READER

sopa de funcho *fennel soup with beans and bacon fat*
sopa de legumes *vegetable soup*
sopa de marisco *shellfish soup*
sopa de pedra *a rich soup with lots of meat, beans and vegetables*
sopa de peixe *fish soup*
sopa de poejos *pennyroyal soup with eggs*
sopa de tomate *tomato soup*
sopa dos campinos *salt cod and tomato soup*
sopa dourada *dessert made with egg yolks*
sopa e um papo-seco *soup and roll*
sopa seca *thick bread soup with meats*
suspiros *meringues*
tamboril *monkfish*
tangerina *mandarin*
tarte de amêndoa *almond tart*
tarte de limão *lemon tart*
tarte de maçã *apple tart*
tibornas *slices of freshly baked bread sprinkled with coarse sea salt and olive oil*
tigeladas de Abrantes *individually baked custards in special cups*
tomate *tomato*
toranja *grapefruit*
torradas *toast*
torta de laranja *orange tart*
torta de Viana *a sponge roll filled with a rich egg sweet*
tostas *toasted sandwiches*
toucinho do céu *'bacon from heaven', an egg and almond pudding*
tripas à moda do Porto *tripe stew with beans and various meats*
truta *trout*
trutas à moda do Minho *trout cooked in wine and rich seasonings*
uvas *grapes*
vinagre *vinegar*
vinha d'alhos *marinated in wine and garlic*
vitela *veal*
vitela no espeto *veal cooked on the spit*

DICTIONARY
english-portuguese
portuguese-english

A

a um (uma)
abbey a abadia
abortion o aborto
abortion pill a pílula abortiva
about cerca de
  about ten o'clock por volta das dez
above acima de; por cima de
abroad *adj* no estrangeiro
  go abroad ir ao estrangeiro
abscess um abcesso
accelerator o acelerador
accent o acento
  (pronunciation) a pronúncia
to accept aceitar ; aprovar
accident o acidente
accommodation o alojamento
account a conta
accountant o/a contabilista
to ache doer
  I have a headache dói-me a cabeça
acid o ácido
actor/actress o actor/a actriz
to adapt adaptar ; ajustar
adaptor *(electrical)* o adaptador
adder a víbora
address a morada
  what is your address? qual é a sua morada?
address book a agenda
admission charge/fee o preço de entrada
adult o/a adulto(a)
  for adults para adultos
advance: *in advance* antecipadamente
advertisement o anúncio
to advise aconselhar
aerial a antena

aeroplane o avião
aerosol o aerossol
to be afraid of ter medo de
after depois
  after lunch depois do almoço
afternoon a tarde
  this afternoon esta tarde
  in the afternoon à tarde
  tomorrow afternoon amanhã à tarde
aftershave o aftershave
again outra vez
against *prep* contra
age a idade
  old age a idade avançada
agency a agencia
ago: *2 days ago* há 2 dias
to agree concordar
agreement o acordo
AIDS a SIDA
airbag o airbag
air conditioning o ar condicionado
  is there airconditioning? tem ar condicionado?
air freshener o purificador do ambiente
airline a linha aérea
air mail a via aérea
air mattress o colchão pneumático
airport o aeroporto
airport bus o autocarro do aeroporto
air ticket o bilhete de avião
aisle *(plane, theatre, etc)* a coxia
alarm o alarme
alarm clock o despertador
alcohol-free sem álcool
alcoholic *adj* alcoólico(a)
all todo(a), todos(as)
allergic alérgico(a)
  I'm allergic to sou alérgico(a) a
allergy a alergia
alley a travessa

to allow permitir
  to be allowed estar permitido
all right está bem
  are you all right? você está bem?
almond a amêndoa
almost quase
alone sozinho(a)
alphabet o alfabeto
also também
altar o altar
always sempre
am see (to be) **GRAMMAR**
ambulance a ambulância
America a América
American americano(a)
amount: *total amount* o total
anaesthetic a anestesia
  general anaesthetic a anestesia geral
  local anaesthetic a anestesia local
anchor a âncora
anchovy a anchova
ancient antigo(a)
and e
angel o anjo
angina a angina de peito
angry zangado(a)
animal um animal
aniseed a erva-doce
ankle o tornozelo
anniversary o aniversário
annual anual
another um(a) outro(a)
  another beer? mais uma cerveja?
answer *n* a resposta
to answer responder
answerphone o gravador de chamadas
ant a formiga
antacid o antiácido
antibiotic o antibiótico

antifreeze o anticongelante
antihistimine o anti-histamínico
antiques as antiguidades
antique shop a loja de antiguidades
antiseptic o antiséptico
any: *have you any apples?* tem maçãs?
apartment o apartamento
aperitif o aperitivo
appendicitis a apendicite
apple a maçã
application form o formulário de requerimento
appointment *(meeting)* o encontro
  (doctor) a consulta
  (hairdresser) a hora marcada
apricot o damasco
are see (to be) **GRAMMAR**
arm o braço
armbands *(to swim)* as braçadeiras
armchair a poltrona
aromatherapy a aromaterapia
to arrange organizar
to arrest prender
arrival a chegada
to arrive chegar
art gallery a galeria de arte
arthritis a artrite
artichoke a alcachofra
artist o/a artista
ashtray o cinzeiro
to ask *(question)* perguntar
  (to ask for something) pedir
asparagus o espargo
aspirin a aspirina
  soluble aspirin aspirina efervescente
asthma a asma
at em
  at home em casa
  at 8 o'clock às oito
  at once imediatamente

at night à noite
Atlantic Ocean o oceano Atlântico
to attack atacar
attractive *(person)* atraente
aubergine a beringela
auction o leilão
audience a audiência
August Agosto
aunt a tia
au pair o/a au pair
Australia a Austrália
Australian australiano(a)
author o autor/a autora
automatic car o carro automático
auto-teller o caixa automático
autumn o outono
available disponível
avenue a avenida
avocado o abacate
to avoid evitar
awful terrível
axle o eixo

B

baby o bebé
baby food a comida de bebé
baby milk o leite infantil
baby's bottle o biberão
baby seat *(in car)* o assento do bebé
baby-sitter o/a babysitter
baby wipes as toalhitas
bachelor o solteiro
back *(of body)* as costas
  back ache a dor de costas
  back seat o assento traseiro
backpack a mochila
bacon o toucinho
bad *(weather, news)* má (mau)
  (fruit, vegetables) podre

bag o saco ; a mala
baggage a bagagem
baggage allowance o peso limite da bagagem
baggage reclaim a recolha de bagagem
bait *(for fishing)* a isca
baked assado
baker's a padaria
balcony a varanda
bald *(person)* calvo(a)
  (tyre) careca
ball a bola
ballet o ballet
balloon o balão
banana a banana
band *(music)* a banda musical
bandage a ligadura
bank o banco
  (river) a margem
bar o bar
barbeque o churrasco
  to have a barbecue fazer um churrasco
barber o barbeiro
basket o cesto
basketwork os cestos ; os artigos de vime
bath o banho
  to take a bath tomar banho
bathing cap a touca de banho
bathroom a casa de banho
  with bathroom com casa de banho
battery *(for car)* a bateria
  (for torch, radio, etc) a pilha
bay leaf a folha de louro
to be see (to be) **GRAMMAR**
beach a praia
bean o feijão
  broad bean a fava
  french/green bean o feijão verde

b

kidney bean o feijão encarnado
soya bean o feijão de soja
bear *(animal)* o urso
beard a barba
beautiful belo(a)
bed a cama
  double bed a cama de casal
  single bed a cama de solteiro
  sofa bed o sofá-cama
  twin beds as camas separadas
bedding a roupa de cama
bedroom o quarto
bee a abelha
beef a carne de vaca
beer a cerveja
beetroot a beterraba
before antes de
  before breakfast antes do
  pequeno-almoço
beggar o/a mendigo(a)

b

to begin começar
behind atrás
  behind the bank atrás do banco
beige bege
to believe acreditar
bell *(door)* a campainha
  (church) o sino
below por baixo de
belt o cinto
bend *(in road)* a curva
berth *(in ship)* o beliche
beside *(next to)* ao lado de
  beside the bank ao lado do
  banco
best o/a melhor
to bet on apostar em
better (than) melhor (do que)
between entre
bib o bibe
bicycle a bicicleta
  by bicycle de bicicleta
bicycle lock o cadeado da bicicleta
bicycle repair kit o estojo de fer-

b

ramentas
bidet o bidé
big grande
bigger (than) maior que
bike *(pushbike)* a bicicleta
  mountain bike a bicicleta de
  montanha
bikini o bikini
bill a conta
bin o caixote do lixo
bin liner o saco do lixo
binoculars os binóculos
bird o pássaro
biro a esferográfica
birth certificate a certidão de
nascimento
birthday o aniversário
  happy birthday parabéns
  my birthday is on... faço anos
  no...
birthday card o cartão de
aniversário
birthday present a prenda de
anos
biscuits as bolachas
bit: *a bit of* um bocado (de)
bite *(insect)* a picada ; a mordedura
bitten *(animal)* mordido(a)
  (insect) picado(a)
bitter amargo(a)
black preto(a)
blackberry a amora silvestre
blackcurrant a groselha
blank o espaço vazio/em branco
blanket o cobertor
bleach a lixívia
to bleed sangrar
blender *(for food)* a liquidificadora
blind *(person)* cego(a)
blind *(for window)* a persiana
blister a bolha
blocked bloqueado(a), entupido (a)
blood o sangue

blood group o grupo sanguíneo
blood test a análise ao sangue
blouse a blusa
blow-dry o brushing
blue azul
  dark blue azul-escuro
  light blue azul-claro
blunt *(knife, etc)* embotado(a)
boarding card o cartão de embarque
boarding house a pensão
boat o barco
boat trip a viagem de barco
body o corpo
to boil ferver
boiled cozido(a)
bone o osso
book o livro
  book of tickets a caderneta de bilhetes
to book reservar
booking a marcação
booking office a bilheteira
bookshop a livraria
boot *(of car)* o porta-bagagem
boots as botas
border a fronteira
boring aborrecido(a)
boss o/a chefe ; o patrão/a patroa
both ambos(as)
bottle a garrafa
  a half bottle uma meia-garrafa
bottle-opener o abre-garrafas
box a caixa
box office a bilheteira
boxer shorts os boxers
boy o rapaz
boyfriend o namorado
bra o soutien
bracelet a pulseira
brain o cérebro
to brake travar

brake fluid o óleo dos travões
brakes os travões
branch *(of tree)* o ramo
  (of business, etc) a sucursal
brand *(make)* a marca
brandy o conhaque
brass o latão
bread o pão
  french bread o cacete
  sliced bread o pão em fatias
  wholemeal bread o pão integral
breadcrumbs pão ralado
bread roll o papo-seco
to break quebrar
breakable frágil
breakdown *(car)* a avaria
breakdown service o pronto-socorro
breakfast o pequeno-almoço
breast *(chicken)* o peito
to breathe respirar
brick o tijolo
bride a noiva
bridge a ponte
  (game) o brídege
briefcase a pasta
bright brilhante
brine a salmoura
to bring trazer
Britain a Grã-Bretanha
British britânico(a)
broad largo(a)
broccoli os brócolos
brochure a brochura
broken partido(a)
broken down *(car, etc)* avariado(a)
bronchitis a bronquite
bronze o bronze
brooch o broche
broom a vassoura
brother o irmão
brother-in-law o cunhado

brown castanho(a)
bruise a nódoa negra
brush a escova
Brussels sprouts as couves-de-Bruxelas
bubble bath a espuma para o banho
bucket o balde
buffet car o vagão restaurante
to build construir
building site a obra
building o edifício
bulb (light) a lâmpada
bumbag a carteira de cintura
bumper (on car) o pára-choques
bunch (of flowers) o ramo
   (of grapes) o cacho
bungee jumping o bungee jumping
bureau de change a casa de câmbio

burger um hambúrguer
burglar o ladrão
burglary o roubo
to burn queimar
burnt (food) queimado
burst rebentado(a)
bus o autocarro
bus station a estação de autocarros
bus stop a paragem de autocarros
bus ticket o bilhete de autocarro
bus tour a excursão de autocarro
business os negócios
   on business de negócios
business card o cartão-de-visita
business class a classe executiva
businessman/woman o homem/a mulher de negócios
business trip a viagem de negócios

busy ocupado(a)
but mas
butcher's o talho
butter a manteiga

button o botão
to buy comprar
by perto de ; por
   (next to) ao lado de
   by bus de autocarro
   by car de carro
   by train de comboio
bypass o desvio

C

cab (taxi) o táxi
caberet o cabaré
cabbage a couve
cabin (on boat) o camarote
cable TV a televisão por cabo
café o café
cafetière a cafeteira
cake o bolo
cake shop a pastelaria
calamine lotion a loção de calamina
calculator a calculadora
calendar o calendário
calf (young cow) o vitelo
to call chamar
call (telephone) uma chamada
   a long-distance call uma chamada interurbana
camcorder a camcorder
camera a máquina fotográfica
camera case o estojo da máquina fotográfica
to camp acampar
camp site o parque de campismo
to can (to be able) poder
can a lata
   canned goods as conservas
can opener o abre-latas
Canada o Canadá
Canadian canadiano(a)
to cancel cancelar
cancellation o cancelamento

cancer o cancro
candle a vela
canoe a canoa
cap *(hat)* o boné
  (diaphragm) o diafragma
capital *(city)* a capital
cappuccino o cappuccino
car o carro
car alarm o alarme do carro
car hire o aluguer de automóveis
car insurance o seguro de automóveis
car keys as chaves do carro
car park o parque de estacionamento
car radio o rádio do carro
car seat *(for children)* o banco para crianças
car wash a lavagem automática
carafe a garrafa ; o jarro
caravan a caravana
carburettor o carburador
card *(greetings)* o cartão
  (playing) a carta de jogar
careful cuidadoso(a)
  be careful! cuidado!
carnation o cravo
carpet a carpete
  (rug) o tapete
carriage a carruagem
carrot a cenoura
to carry transportar
case *(suitcase)* a mala
cash o dinheiro
to cash *(cheque)* levantar
cash desk a caixa
cash dispenser o caixa automático
cashier o/a caixa
cassette a cassette
cassette player o gravador
castle o castelo
cat o gato

catalogue o catálogo
to catch *(bus, train, etc)* apanhar
cathedral a catedral
Catholic católico(a)
cauliflower a couve-flor
cave a caverna
CD o disco compacto
CD player o leitor de discos compactos
ceiling o tecto
celery o aipo
cellar a cave
cemetery o cemitério
centimetre o centímetro
central central
central heating o aquecimento central
central locking o fecho centralizado
centre o centro
century o século
  19th century o século dezanove
  21st century o século vinte e um
ceramics a cerâmica
certain certo(a)
certificate o certificado
chain a corrente
chair a cadeira
chambermaid a empregada de quarto
Champagne o champanhe
change *(loose coins)* o dinheiro trocado
  (money returned) o troco
to change trocar ; mudar
  to change money trocar dinheiro
  to change (clothes) mudar de roupa
  to change (train, etc) mudar
changing room o gabinete de provas

C

Channel o Canal da Mancha
chapel a capela
charcoal o carvão
charge o custo
  cover charge o couvert
charter flight o voo charter
cheap barato(a)
cheaper mais barato(a)
to check verificar
to check in *(at airport)* fazer o check-in
  (at hotel) apresentar-se
check-in desk o balcão do check-in
cheerful bem disposto(a) ; alegre
cheers saúde!
cheese o queijo
cheeseburger um hambúrger com queijo
chef o/a chefe, cozinheiro(a)
chemist's a farmácia
cheque o cheque
cheque book o livro de cheques
cheque card o cartão de cheques
cherry a cereja
chest *(of body)* o peito
chestnut a castanha
chewing gum a pastilha elástica
chicken a galinha
chickenpox a varicela
child a criança
children as crianças
chilli a malagueta
chimney a chaminé
chin o queixo
china a porcelana
chips as batatas fritas
chocolate o chocolate
chocolates os chocolates
choir o coro
chop *(meat)* a costeleta
chopping board a tábua da cozinha

christening o baptizado
Christmas o Natal
  merry Christmas! feliz Natal!
Christmas card o cartão de Boas Festas!
Christmas Eve a véspera de Natal
Christmas present a prenda de Natal
church a igreja
cider a cidra
cigar o charuto
cigarette o cigarro
cigarette lighter o isqueiro
cigarette papers as mortalhas
cinema o cinema
circle *(theatre)* o balcão
circuit breaker o disjuntor
circus o circo
cistern a cisterna
citizen o cidadão/a cidadã
city a cidade
claim a reclamação
to clap bater palmas
class: first class primeira classe
  second class segunda classe
clean limpo(a)
to clean limpar
cleanser o leite de limpeza
clear claro(a)
client o/a cliente
cliff o rochedo
to climb subir
climbing o alpinismo
climbing boots as botas de alpinismo
clingfilm® a película aderente
clinic a clínica
cloakroom o vestiário
clock o relógio
to close fechar
closed fechado(a)

cloth *(fabric)* o tecido
(rag) o trapo
clothes as roupas
clothes line o estendal
clothes peg a mola da roupa
clothes shop as roupas
cloudy nublado(a)
clove *(spice)* o cravinho
club o clube
clutch a embraiagem
coach o autocarro
coach station a rodoviária
coach trip a viagem de autocarro
coal o carvão
coast a costa ; o litoral
coastguard a polícia marítima
coat o casaco
coat hanger o cabide
Coca Cola® a Coca-Cola®
cockroach a barata
cocktail o cocktail
cocoa o cacau
coconut o coco
cod o bacalhau
code o código
coffee o café
white coffee o café com leite
black coffee o café
decaffeinated coffee o café
descafeinado
coil *(contraceptive)* o DIU
coin a moeda
Coke® a Coca-Cola®
colander o coador
cold frio(a)
I'm cold tenho frio
cold water a água fria
cold *(illness)* a constipação
I have a cold tenho uma
constipação
cold sore a herpes labial
collar *(of dress)* a gola
(of shirt) o colarinho

collar bone a clavícula
colleague o/a colega
to collect coleccionar
colour a cor
colour blind daltónico(a)
colour film *(for camera)* o rolo a
cores
comb o pente
to come vir ; chegar
to come back voltar
to come in entrar
come in! entre!
comedy a comédia
comfortable confortável
company *(firm)* a companhia
compartment o compartimento
compass a bússola
to complain queixar-se (de)
complaint uma queixa
composer um compositor
compulsory obrigatório(a)
computer o computador
computer disk *(floppy)* uma disquete
computer game o jogo de computador
computer software o software
concert o concerto
concert hall a sala de concertos
concession o desconto
concussion o traumatismo craniano
condition *(requirement)* a condição
(state) o estado
conditioner o amaciador
condom o preservativo
conference a conferência
confession a confissão
to confirm confirmar
please confirm é favor confirmar
confirmation *(of booking)* a confir-
mação
congratulations! parabéns!
connection *(flight, etc)* a ligação

C

constipated com prisão de ventre
consulate o consulado
contact lens cleaner o líquido para as lentes de contacto
contact lenses as lentes de contacto
to continue continuar
contraceptive o preservativo; o anticoncepcional
contract o contrato
convenient: is it convenient? é conveniente?
to cook cozinhar
cooked cozinhado(a)
cooker o fogão
cool fresco(a)
cool box *(for picnics)* a caixa refrigerada
copper cobre
copy a cópia
to copy copiar
coriander os coentros
cork *(in bottle)* a rolha
corkscrew o saca-rolhas
corner o canto
corridor o corredor
cortisone a cortisona
cost o custo
to cost custar
how much does it cost? quanto é que custa?
cot o berço
cottage a casa de campo
cotton o algodão
cotton buds os cotonetes
cotton wool o algodão (hidrófilo)
couchette a couchette
to cough tossir
cough a tosse
cough mixture o xarope para a tosse
cough sweets as pastilhas para a tosse

counter *(shop, bar, etc)* a balcão
country o país
countryside o campo
couple o casal
courier *(tour guide)* o guia turístico
courier service o mensageiro
course *(of meal)* o prato *(of study)* o curso
cousin primo(a)
cover charge o couvert
cow a vaca
crab o caranguejo
craftsman/woman o artesão/a artesã
cramps as cãibras
crash *(car)* o choque
to crash colidir
crash helmet o capacete
cream *(for face, etc)* o creme *(on milk)* a nata
soured cream as natas azedas
whipped cream o chantilly
credit card o cartão de crédito
crime o crime
crisps as batatinhas fritas
crop a colheita
croissant o croissant
to cross *(road)* cruzar
crossed lines as linhas cruzadas
crossing *(sea)* a travessia
crossroads a encruzilhada
crossword puzzle as palavras cruzadas
crowd a multidão
crowded cheio(a) de gente
crown a coroa
cruise o cruzeiro
crutches as muletas
to cry *(weep)* chorar
crystal o cristal
cucumber o pepino
cufflinks os botões de punho

cul-de-sac o beco sem saída
cumin o cominho
cup a chávena
cupboard o aparador ; o armário
currant a passa de corinto
currency a moeda
current a corrente
curtain a cortina
cushion a almofada
custard o leite-creme
custom *(tradition)* o costume
customer o freguês/a freguesa
to cut cortar
  we've been cut off foi inter-
  rompida a ligação
cutlery os talheres
to cycle andar de bicicleta
cycle track a pista para ciclistas
cyst o quisto
cystitis a cistite

D

daffodil o narciso
daily cada dia
dairy produce os lacticínios
daisy a margarida
damage os danos
damp húmido(a)
dance o baile
to dance dançar
danger o perigo
dangerous perigoso(a)
dark escuro(a)
  after dark depois do anoitecer
date a data
date of birth a data de nascimento
daughter a filha
daughter-in-law a nora
dawn a madrugada
day o dia
  every day todos os dias

  per day ao dia
dead morto(a)
deaf surdo(a)
dear *(on letter)* querido(a)
  (expensive) caro(a)
death a morte
debt a dívida
decaffeinated coffee o café
  descafeinado
  have you decaff? tem café
  descafeinado?
December Dezembro
deck chair a cadeira de lona
to declare: *nothing to declare*
  nada a declarar
deep fundo(a)
deep freeze o congelador
to defrost descongelar
to de-ice descongelar
delay a demora
  how long is the delay? quanto
  é o atraso?
delayed atrasado(a)
delicatessen a charcutaria
delicious delicioso(a)
dental floss fio dental
dentist o/a dentista
dentures a dentadura postiça
deodorant o desodorizante
department store o grande
  armazém
departure lounge a sala de
  embarque
departures as partidas
deposit o depósito
to describe descrever
description a descrição
desk *(in hotel, airport)* o balcão
dessert a sobremesa
details os pormenores
detergent o detergente
detour o desvio
to develop desenvolver

diabetes a diabetes
diabetic diabético(a)
  I'm diabetic sou diabético(a)
to dial marcar
dialling code o código
dialling tone o sinal
diamond o diamante
diapers as fraldas
diarrhoea a diarreia
diary o diário
dice os dados
dictionary o dicionário
to die morrer
diesel o gasóleo
diet a dieta
  I'm on a diet estou de dieta
different diferente
difficult difícil
dinghy o bote
dining room a sala de jantar
dinner o jantar
  to have dinner jantar
diplomat o diplomata
direct directo(a)
directions *(instructions)*
  instrucções
  to ask for directions pedir indi-
  cações
directory *(phone)* a lista telefónica
directory enquiries as informações
  telefónicas
dirty sujo(a)
disabled *(person)* o/a deficiente
to disappear desaparecer
disappointed desiludido(a)
disaster o desastre
disco a discoteca
to discover descobrir
discount o desconto
disease a doença
dish o prato
dishwasher a máquina de lavar
  louça

dishwasher powder o detergente em pó
disinfectant o desinfectante
disk *(computer)* o disco
  floppy disk a disquete
  hard disk o disco duro
to dislocate *(joint)* deslocar
distant distante
distilled water a água destilada
district o distrito
to disturb incomodar
to dive mergulhar
diversion o desvio
divorced divorciado(a)
  I'm divorced sou divorciado(a)
DIY shop a loja de bricolaje
dizzy tonto(a)
to do fazer *see* GRAMMAR
doctor o/a médico(a)
documents os documentos
dog *(male)* o cão
  (female) a cadela
doll a boneca
dollar o dólar
domestic flight o voo doméstico
dominoes o dominó
donor card o cartão de dador
donkey o burro
door a porta
double o dobro
double bed a cama de casal
double room o quarto de casal
doughnut a bola de Berlim
down: to go down descer
downstairs em baixo
dragonfly a libélula
drain o cano ; o esgoto
draught *(of air)* a corrente de ar
  there's a draught há uma corrente de ar
draught lager a imperial
drawer a gaveta
drawing o desenho

dress o vestido
to dress (oneself) vestir-se
dressing *(for food)* o tempero ; o molho
dressing gown o roupão
drill *(tool)* a broca
drink a bebida
to drink beber
drinking chocolate o chocolate
drinking water a água potável
to drive conduzir
driver o/a condutor(a)
driving licence a carta de condução
drizzle o chuvisco
drought a seca
to drown afogar
drug *(medicine)* o medicamento *(narcotic)* a droga
drunk bêbedo(a)
dry seco(a)
to dry secar
dry-cleaner's a limpeza a seco
dryer o secador
duck o pato
due: when is it due está previsto para quando?
dummy *(for baby)* a chupeta
during durante
dust o pó
to dust limpar o pó
duster o pano do pó
duvet o edredão
duvet cover o saco do edredão
dye a tinta
dynamo o dínamo

E

each cada
eagle a águia
ear a orelha

earache a dor de ouvidos
  I have earache doem-me os ouvidos
earlier mais cedo
early cedo
ear-phones os auscultadores
earrings os brincos
earth *(planet)* a terra
earthquake o terramoto
east o leste
Easter a Páscoa
easy fácil
to eat comer
ebony o ébano
echo o eco
edge a beira ; a aresta
eel a enguia
effective eficaz
egg o ovo
  fried egg o ovo estrelado
  hard-boiled egg o ovo cozido
  scrambled eggs os ovos mexidos
  soft-boiled egg o ovo quente
egg white a clara de ovo
egg yolk a gema de ovo
either... or... ou... ou...
elastic band o elástico
elastoplast o penso
elbow o cotovelo
electric eléctrico(a)
electrician o/a electricista
electricity a electricidade
electricity meter o contador de electricidade
electric razor a máquina de barbear
electric shock o choque eléctrico
elevator o elevador
elegant elegante
e-mail o correio electrónico
e-mail address o endereço de correio electrónico
embarrassing embaraçoso(a)

e

e

embassy a embaixada
emergency a emergência
emergency exit a saída de
  emergência
empty vazio(a)
end o fim
engaged comprometido(a)
  (phone, toilet, etc) ocupado(a)
engine o motor
engineer o/a engenheiro(a)
England a Inglaterra
English inglês (inglesa)
  (language) o inglês
enjoy oneself divertir-se
  I enjoy swimming gosto de nadar
  I enjoy dancing gosto de dançar
  enjoy yourself! diverte-te!
to enlarge aumentar
enormous enorme
enough bastante
  that's enough chega
enquiry desk o balcão de
  informações
to enter entrar
enthusiastic entusiástico(a)
entertainment a diversão
entrance a entrada
entrance fee o bilhete de entrada
envelope o envelope
epileptic epiléptico
epileptic fit o ataque epiléptico
equipment o equipamento
eraser a borracha
error o erro
escalator a escada rolante
to escape escapar ; fugir
escape ladder a escada de
  salvação
espadrilles as alpercatas
essential essencial
estate agent's o agente imobi-
  liário
establish estabelecer

Euro o Euro
Eurocheque o Eurocheque
Europe a Europa
eve a véspera
  Christmas Eve a véspera de Natal
  New Year's Eve a véspera de
  Ano Novo
even *(number)* par
evening a noite
  in the evening à noite
evening dress o traje de cerimónia
evening meal o jantar
every cada
everyone toda a gente
everything todas as coisas, tudo
everywhere por todo o lado
examination o exame
example: *for example* por exemplo
excellent excelente
except excepto
excess luggage o excesso de
  bagagem
to exchange trocar
exchange rate o câmbio
exciting excitante
excursion a excursão
excuse a desculpa
  excuse me! desculpe!
exercise *(physical)* o exercício
exercise book o caderno
exhaust pipe o tubo de escape
exhibition a exposição
exit a saída
expenses as despesas
expensive caro(a)
expert o/a perito(a)
to expire *(ticket, etc)* caducar
to explain explicar
explosion a explosão
to export exportar
express *(train)* o expresso
express: *to send a letter express*

mandar uma carta por correio expresso
extension *(electrical)* a extensão
extra extra
to extinguish apagar
eye o olho
eyebrows as sobrancelhas
eye drops as gotas para os olhos
eyelashes as pestanas
eyeliner o lápis para os olhos

F

fabric o tecido
face a cara
face cloth toalha de rosto
facial a limpeza facial
factory a fábrica
to faint desmaiar
fainted desmaiado(a)
fair *(hair)* louro(a)
fair *(funfair)* a feira
fairway *(golf)* o fairway
fake falso(a)
fall *(autumn)* o Outono
to fall cair
  he/she has fallen ele/ela caiu
false teeth os dentes postiços
family a família
famous famoso(a)
fan *(hand-held)* o leque
  (electric) a ventoinha
  (football, jazz) o/a fan
fan belt a correia da ventoinha
far longe
  is it far? é longe?
fare *(train, bus, etc)* o preço (da passagem)
farm a quinta
farmer o/a agricultor(a)
fashionable de moda
fast rápido(a)
  too fast rápido demais

to fasten *(seatbelt)* apertar
fat gordo(a)
father o pai
father-in-law o sogro
fault *(defect)* o defeito
  it's not my fault a culpa não é minha
favourite favorito(a)
fax o fax
to fax mandar por fax
fax number o número de fax
feather a pena
February Fevereiro
to feed alimentar
to feel apalpar ; sentir
  I feel sick tenho náuseas
  I don't feel well sinto-me mal-disposto(a)
feet os pés
fellow o companheiro
felt-tip pen a caneta de feltro
female mulher
ferry o ferry-boat
festival o festival
to fetch *(to bring)* trazer
  (to go and get) ir buscar
fever a febre
few poucos(as)
  a few alguns (algumas)
fiancé(e) o/a noivo(a)
field o campo
fig o figo
fight a briga
file *(computer)* o ficheiro
  (nail) a lima
filigree a filigrana
to fill encher
  fill it up! encha o depósito!
  to fill in *(form)* preencher
fillet o filete
film *(at cinema)* o filme
  (for camera) o rolo de películas
  colour film o rolo a cores

f

f

f

115

f

black and white film o rolo a preto e branco
filofax® a agenda
filter o filtro
to find achar
fine *(to be paid)* a multa
fine fino(a)
  fine arts as belas-artes
finger o dedo
to finish acabar
fire o fogo
fire alarm o alarme contra incêndios
fire brigade os bombeiros
fire engine o carro dos bombeiros
fire escape a saída de incêndios
fire extinguisher o extintor
fireplace a lareira
fireworks os fogos de artifício

f

first o/a primeiro(a)
first aid os primeiros socorros
first aid kit o estojo de primeiros socorros
first class a primeira classe
first floor o primeiro andar
first name o nome próprio
fish o peixe
to fish pescar
fisherman o pescador
fishing permit a licença de pesca
fishing rod a cana de pesca
fishmonger's a peixaria
to fit: *it doesn't fit me* não me serve
fit o ataque
  he had a fit ele teve um ataque
to fix reparar
  can you fix it? pode arranjá-lo?

f

fizzy gasoso(a)
flag a bandeira
flash *(for camera)* o flash
flashlight a lanterna

flask o termo
flat *(apartment)* o apartamento
flat plano(a)
  (battery) descarregado
  this drink is flat esta bebida já perdeu o gás
flat tyre o furo
flavour sabor
  which flavour? de que sabor?
flaw a falha
fleas as pulgas
fleece *(top/jacket)* de fibra polar
flex o cabo eléctrico
flight o voo
flip flops os chinelos
flippers as barbatanas
flood a inundação
floor o chão
  (storey) o andar
  which floor? qual é o andar?
  ground floor o rés-do-chão
floorcloth o pano do chão
floppy disk a disquete
florist's shop a florista
flour a farinha
flower a flor
flu a gripe
fly a mosca
to fly voar
fly sheet o duplo-tecto
fog o nevoeiro
foggy enevoado(a)
foil *(silver)* o papel de alumínio
to follow seguir
food a comida
food poisoning a intoxicação alimentar
fool tonto(a)
foot o pé
  on foot a pé
football o futebol
football match o jogo de futebol
football pitch o campo de futebol

football player o jogador de futebol
footpath o caminho
for para
  for me para mim
  for you para si
  for him/her/us para ele/ela/nós
forbidden proibido(a)
forehead a testa
foreign estrangeiro(a)
foreigner o/a estrangeiro(a)
forecast a previsão
  weather forecast a previsão do tempo
forest a floresta
forever para sempre
to forget esquecer-se de
to forgive perdoar
fork *(for eating)* o garfo
  (in road) a bifurcação
form *(document)* o formulário
formal dress o traje de cerimónia
fortnight a quinzena
fortress a fortaleza
forward(s) para a frente
foul *(in football)* a falta
fountain a fonte
four-wheel drive o quatro-vezes-quatro
fox a raposa
fracture a fractura
fragile frágil
frame *(picture)* a moldura
France a França
free *(not occupied)* livre
  (costing nothing) grátis
freezer o congelador
French francês (francesa)
  (language) o francês
french beans o feijão-verde
french fries as batatas fritas
frequent frequente
fresh fresco(a)

fresh water a água doce
Friday Sexta-feira
fridge o frigorífico
fried frito(a)
friend o/a amigo(a)
frog a rã
from de
  from England da Inglaterra
  from Scotland da Escócia
front a frente
  in front of em frente de
front door a porta da frente
frost a geada
frozen congelado(a)
fruit a fruta
  dried fruit frutos secos
fruit juice o sumo de frutas
fruit salad a salada de frutas
to fry fritar
frying pan a frigideira
fuel *(petrol)* a gasolina
fuel pump a bomba de gasolina
full cheio(a)
full board a pensão completa
fumes *(of car)* os fumos de escape
fun a diversão
funeral o funeral
funfair o parque de diversões
funny engraçado(a) ; estranho(a)
fur a pele
furnished mobilado
furniture a mobília
fuse o fusível
fuse box a caixa de fusíveis
futon o futon
future o futuro

G

gallery *(art)* a galeria de arte
gallon = approx. 4.5 litres
game o jogo

g

(animal) a caça
garage a garagem
   (for repairs) a oficina
garden o jardim
gardener o/a jardineiro(a)
garlic o alho
garnish vb guarnecer
gas o gás
gas cooker o fogão a gas
gas cylinder a botija de gás
gate (airport) a porta
gear a velocidade
   first gear a primeira
   second gear a segunda
   third gear a terceira
   fourth gear a quarta
   neutral o ponto morto
   reverse a marcha atrás
gearbox a caixa de velocidades
generous generoso(a)
gents' (toilet) homens
genuine autêntico(a)
German alemão (alemã)
   (language) o alemão
German measles a rubéola
Germany a Alemanha
to get (to obtain) obter
   (to receive) receber
   (to fetch) ir buscar
to get into entrar
to get off descer de
gift o presente
gift shop a loja de lembranças
gin and tonic um gim tónico
ginger o gengibre
girl a rapariga
girlfriend a namorada
to give dar
to give back devolver
glass (to drink out of) o copo
   a glass of water um copo de
   água
glasses os óculos

gloss o lustro ; o brilho
gloves as luvas
glue a cola
to go ir
   I'm going to... vou para...
   we're going to... vamos para...
   to go home voltar para casa
to go back voltar
to go down descer
to go in entrar
to go out sair
goat a cabra
God o Deus
godchild o/a afilhado(a)
goggles os óculos protectores
gold o ouro
golf o golfe
golf ball a bola de golfe
golf clubs os tacos de golfe
golf course o campo de golfe
good bom (boa)
   very good muito bom
good afternoon boa tarde
goodbye adeus
good evening boa noite
good morning bom dia
good night boa noite
goose o ganso
gooseberry a groselha branca
Gothic gótico(a)
graduate o/a licenciado(a)
gram o grama
granddaughter a neta
grandfather o avô
   great grandfather o bisavô
grandmother a avó
   great grandmother a bisavó
grapefruit a toranja
grapefruit juice o sumo de
toranja
grapes as uvas
   green grapes a uva branca
   black grapes a uva preta

grass a erva
grated *(cheese, etc)* ralado(a)
grater *(for cheese, etc)* o ralador
greasy oleoso(a) ; gorduroso(a)
great grande
green verde
green card *(car insurance)* o cartão verde
greengrocer's a frutaria
greetings card o cartão de felicitações
grey cinzento(a)
to grill grelhar
grilled grelhado(a)
grocer's a mercearia
ground *(earth)* a terra
(floor) o chão
ground floor o rés-do-chão
on the ground floor... no rés-do-chão...
group o grupo
to grow crescer
guarantee a garantia
guard o guarda
guest o/a convidado(a)
(in hotel) o/a hóspede
guesthouse a pensão
guide o/a guia
to guide guiar
guidebook a guia
guided tour a excursão guiada
guitar a guitarra
gun a pistola
gym shoes os ténis

H

haberdasher's a retrosaria
haddock o eglefim
haemorrhoids as hemorróidas
hail o granizo
hair o cabelo

hairbrush a escova de cabelo
haircut o corte de cabelo
hairdresser o/a cabeleireiro(a)
hairdryer o secador de cabelo
hair dye a tinta para o cabelo
hair gel o gel para o cabelo
hairgrip o gancho de cabelo
hair mousse a espuma para o cabelo
hair spray a laca
hake a pescada
half a metade
a half bottle of meia garrafa de
half board a meia pensão
half-price pela metade do preço
ham o presunto
hamburger o hambúrguer
hammer o martelo
hand a mão
handbag o saco de mão
handicapped *(person)* o/a deficiente
handkerchief o lenço
handle *(of cup)* a asa
(of door) a maçaneta
handlebars os guiadores
hand luggage a bagagem de mão
hand-made feito(a) à mão
handsome bonito(a), giro(a)
to hang up *(phone)* desligar
hanger o cabide
hang gliding a asa-delta
hangover a ressaca
to happen acontecer
what happened? o que aconteceu?
happy feliz
happy birthday parabéns
harbour o porto
hard duro(a)
(difficult) difícil
hard disk o disco duro

119

hardware shop a loja de ferragens
hare a lebre
harm o mal ; o dano
harvest a colheita
hat o chapéu
to have ter *see* **GRAMMAR**
  I have... eu tenho...
  I don't have... eu não tenho...
  we have... nós temos...
  we don't have... nós não temos...
  do you have...? tem...?
to have to ter que
hay fever a febre dos fenos
hazelnut a avelã
he ele *see* **GRAMMAR**
head a cabeça
headache a dor de cabeça
  I have a headache dói-me a cabeça
headlights os faróis
headphones os auscultadores
head waiter o chefe de mesa
health food shop a loja de produtos dietéticos
to hear ouvir
hearing aid o aparelho auditivo
heart o coração
heart attack o ataque de coração
heartburn a azia
to heat up aquecer
heater o aquecedor
heating o aquecimento
heaven o Céu
heavy pesado(a)
heel *(of foot)* o calcanhar
  (of shoe) o salto
height a altura
helicopter o helicóptero
hello olá
  (on phone) está
help a ajuda

help! socorro!
to help ajudar
  can you help me? pode-me ajudar?
hem a bainha
hen a galinha
hepatitis a hepatite
her seu (sua)
herb a erva aromática
herbal tea a tisana
here aqui
  here is... aqui está...
  here is my passport aqui está o meu passaporte
hernia a hérnia
hi! olá!
to hide *(something)* esconder
  (oneself) esconder-se
high alto(a)
high blood pressure a tensão alta
highchair a cadeira de bebé
high tide a maré-alta
hill a colina
hill-walking o alpinismo
hip a anca
hip replacement a prótese de anca
to hire alugar
his seu (sua)
historic histórico(a)
history a história
to hit bater
to hitchhike andar à boleia
HIV o vírus da SIDA
HIV positive seropositivo(a)
hobby o passatempo
to hold *(to contain)* conter
hold-up o engarrafamento
hole o buraco
holiday o feriado
  on holiday de férias
holy santo(a)
hollow oco(a)

home a casa
  at home em casa
homeopathy a homeopatia
homesick: *to be homesick* ter saudades de casa
  I'm homesick tenho saudades de casa
homosexual homossexual
honest honesto(a)
honey o mel
honeymoon a lua-de-mel
hood *(of jacket)* o capuz
  (of car) a capota
to hope esperar
  I hope so/not espero que sim/não
horn *(of car)* a buzina
hors d'œuvre a entrada
horse o cavalo
horse racing as corridas de cava-lo
hosepipe a mangueira
hospital o hospital
hostel a pousada
hot quente
  I'm hot tenho calor
  it's hot está calor
hot chocolate o chocolate quente
hotel o hotel
hot water a água quente
hot-water bottle o saco de água quente
hour a hora
  half an hour meia-hora
house a casa
housewife/husband a/o dona(o) de casa
house wine o vinho da casa
housework a lida da casa
hovercraft o hovercraft
how como
  how much? quanto?
  how many? quantos(as)?
  how are you? como está?
hundred cem
  five hundred quinhentos
hungry: *I am hungry* tenho fome
hurry: *I'm in a hurry* tenho pressa
to hurt doer
  that hurts isso dói
  my back hurts tenho dor de costas
husband o marido
hut a cabana
hydrofoil o hidrofólio
hypodermic needle a agulha hipodérmica

i

I eu *see* **GRAMMAR**
ice o gelo
  (cube) o cubo
  with ice com gelo
ice box o frigorífico
icecream o gelado
ice lolly o gelado
ice rink o rinque
to ice skate patinar sobre o gelo
ice skates os patins de lâmina
if se
ignition a ignição
ignition key a chave de ignição
ill doente
  I'm ill estou doente
immediately imediatamente
immersion heater o esquentador de imersão
immunisation a imunização
important importante
impossible impossível
in dentro de
  in 10 minutes dentro de dez minutos
  in London em Londres

inch = approx. 2.5 cm
included incluído(a)
to increase aumentar
indigestion a indigestão
indoors em casa
inefficient ineficiente
infectious contagioso(a)
information a informação
ingredient o ingrediente
inhaler *(for medication)* o inalador
injection a injecção
to injure lesionar
injured ferido(a)
ink a tinta
inn a estalagem
inner tube a câmara-de-ar
insect o insecto
insect bite a mordedura de insecto
insect repellent o repelente contra insectos
inside dentro
instalment a prestação
instant coffee o café instantâneo
instead of em vez de
instructor o/a instrutor(a)
insulin a insulina
insurance o seguro
insurance certificate a apólice de seguro
to insure pôr no seguro
insured: *to be insured* estar no seguro
intelligent inteligente
interesting interessante
internet a internet
international internacional
interpreter o/a intérprete
interval o intervalo
interview a entrevista
into em ; dentro
into town ao centro
to introduce to apresentar a

invitation o convite
to invite convidar
invoice a factura
Ireland a Irlanda
Irish irlandês (irlandesa)
iron *(metal)* o ferro
(for clothes) o ferro de engomar
to iron passar a ferro
ironing board a tábua de engomar
ironmonger's a loja de ferragens
is *see* (to be) **GRAMMAR**
island a ilha
it o/a *see* **GRAMMAR**
Italian italiano(a)
(language) o italiano
Italy a Itália
itch a comichão
to itch fazer comichão
item o artigo
itemized bill a factura detalhada
ivory o marfim

J

jack *(for car)* o macaco
jacket o casaco
waterproof jacket o casaco impermeável
jackpot o prémio (de lotaria, rifa)
jacuzzi o jacuzzi
jam a compota
jammed *(stuck)* bloqueado(a)
jar o jarro
jaundice a icterícia
jaw o queixo
jazz o jazz
jealous ciumento(a)
jeans as jeans
jelly a geleia
jellyfish a medusa
jewel a jóia

jewellery a joalharia ; a ourivesaria
job o emprego
to jog ir fazer jogging
joke a piada ; a anedota
journalist o/a jornalista
journey a viagem
judge o juiz/a juíza
jug o jarro
juice o sumo
    apple juice o sumo de maçã
    orange juice o sumo de laranja
    tomato juice o sumo de tomate
    a carton of juice o pacote de
    sumo
July Julho
to jump saltar
jump leads os cabos para ligar a
bateria
junction o cruzamento
June Junho
just: *just two* apenas dois
    I've just arrived acabo de
    chegar

K

karaoke o karaokê
to keep guardar
kennel a casota
kettle a chaleira
key a chave
    card key a chave-cartão
keyring o porta-chaves
kid *(young goat)* o cabrito
kidneys os rins
to kill matar
kilo o quilo
kilometre o quilómetro
kind *(person)* amável
king o rei
kiosk o quiosque
kiss o beijo
to kiss beijar

kitchen a cozinha
kitchen paper o papel de cozinha
kite o papagaio
kitten o/a gatinho(a)
knee o joelho
knee highs as meias até o joelho
knickers as cuecas
knife a faca
to knit fazer malha
to knock *(on door)* bater
to knock down *(with car)* atro-
pelar
to knock over *(vase, glass)* der-
rubar
knot o nó
to know *(have knowledge of)* saber
(person, place) conhecer

L

label a etiqueta
lace a renda
laces *(for shoes)* os atacadores
ladder a escada
ladies' *(toilet)* senhoras
lady a senhora
lager a cerveja
    bottled lager a cerveja de gar-
rafa
    draught lager a imperial
lake o lago
lamb o cordeiro
lamp a lâmpada
lamppost o poste de iluminação
land a terra
    (country) o país
to land aterrar
landing *(of plane)* a aterragem
landlady a senhoria
landlord o senhorio
landslide o desabamento
lane *(on motorway)* a faixa
language a língua

laptop o computador portátil
large grande
last último(a)
  the last bus o último autocarro
  the last train o último comboio
  last night ontem á noite
  last week a semana passada
  last year o ano passado
late tarde
  the train is late a comboio está atrasado
  sorry we are late desculpe o atraso
later mais tarde
launderette a lavandaria automática
laundry service o serviço de lavandaria
lavatory o lavabo
lavender a alfazema
law a lei
lawyer o/a advogado(a)
laxative o laxante
layby a berma
lazy preguiçoso(a)
lead *(electrical)* o cabo
lead *(metal)* o chumbo
leaf a folha
leak a fuga
to learn aprender
lease o arrendamento
least: at least pelo menos
leather o couro ; o cabedal
to leave partir ; deixar
  when does it leave? a que horas parte?
  when does the bus leave? a que horas parte o autocarro?
  when does the train leave? a que horas parte o comboio?
leek o alho francês
left: on/to the left à esquerda
left-handed canhoto(a)
left-luggage *(office)* o depósito

de bagagens
leg a perna
legal legal
lemon o limão
lemonade a limonada
lemon tea o carioca de limão
lend emprestar
length o comprimento
lens a lente
less menos
lesson a lição
let *(allow)* deixar
  (lease) alugar
letter a carta
  (of alphabet) a letra
letterbox o marco do correio
lettuce a alface
library a biblioteca
licence *(driving)* a carta de condução
lid a tampa
lie down deitar-se
life a vida
lifeboat o salva-vidas
lifeguard o banheiro salva-vidas
life jacket o colete de salvação
lift o elevador
light a luz
  have you a light? tem lume?
light bulb a lâmpada
lighter o isqueiro
lightning os relâmpagos
like como
  it's like this é assim
to like gostar de
  I like coffee gosto de café
  I don't like... não gosto de...
  I'd like to... gostava de...
  we'd like to... gostavamos de...
lilo o colchão de ar
lime a lima
line *(row, queue)* a fila
  (phone) a linha*

linen o linho, a roupa de cama
lingerie a roupa interior
lion o leão
lips os lábios
lip salve a manteiga de cacau
lipstick o bâton
liqueur o licor
list a lista
to listen to ouvir
litre o litro
litter *(rubbish)* o lixo
little pequeno(a)
  a little… um pouco de…
to live viver
  I live in Edinburgh moro em Edimburgo
  he lives in London ele vive em Londres
liver o fígado
living room a sala de estar
lizard o lagarto
loaf o pão
lobster a lagosta
local local
to lock fechar com chave
lock a fechadura
  the lock is broken a fechadura está quebrada
  bike lock o cadeado da bicicleta
locker *(luggage)* o depósito de bagagem
log book *(for car)* a documentação do carro
lollipop o chupa-chupa
London Londres
  in London em Londres
  to London a Londres
long comprido(a) ; longo(a)
  for a long time durante muito tempo
long-sighted presbíope
to look after cuidar de
to look at olhar

to look for procurar
loose solto(a)
lorry o camião
to lose perder
lost perdido(a)
  I have lost my wallet perdi a minha carteira
  I am lost perdi-me
lost-property office a secção de perdidos e achados
lot: *a lot* muitos
lotion a loção
lottery a lotaria
loud *(noisy)* ruidoso(a)
  (volume) alto(a)
lounge a sala de estar
to love amar
  I love swimming gosto muito de nadar
lovely encantador(a)
low baixo(a)
low-fat com baixo teor de gordura
low tide a maré-baixa
luck a sorte
lucky: *to be lucky* ter sorte
luggage a bagagem
luggage rack o porta-bagagens
luggage tag a etiqueta de bagagem
luggage trolley o carrinho
lump *(swelling)* o inchaço
  (on head) o galo
lunch o almoço
lung o pulmão
luxury o luxo

M

machine a máquina
madam a senhora
magazine a revista
maggot a larva

m

magnet o íman
magnifying glass a lupa
magpie a pega
maid a empregada
maiden name o nome de solteira
mail o correio
  by mail pelo correio
main principal
main course *(of meal)* o prato principal
mains *(electrical)* a rede eléctrica
to make fazer ; preparar
make-up a maquilhagem
male masculino(a)
man o homem
manager o/a gerente
managing director o/a director(a) geral
many muitos(as)
map o mapa
marathon a maratona
marble o mármore
margarine a margarina
marina a marina
marinated marinado
marjoram a manjerona
mark *(stain)* a nódoa
market o mercado
  where is the market? onde é que fica o mercado?
  when is the market? quando é que há mercado?
marmalade o doce de laranja
married casado(a)
  I'm married sou casado(a)
  are you married? é casado(a)?
marsh o pântano
marzipan o maçapão
mascara o rímel®
mashed potato o puré de batata
mass *(church service)* a missa
mast o mastro
match o fósforo

  (game) o jogo
material o material
to matter: *it doesn't matter* não tem importância
  what is the matter? o que é que se passa?
mattress o colchão
May Maio
mayonnaise a maionese
meadow o prado
meal a refeição
to mean significar
  what does this mean? o que é que isto quer dizer?
measles o sarampo
to measure medir
meat a carne
  white meat as carnes brancas
  red meat as carnes vermelhas
  I don't eat meat não como carne
mechanic o/a mecânico(a)
medical insurance seguro de doença
medicine o medicamento
medieval medieval
Mediterranean o Mediterrâneo
medium médio(a)
  medium rare (meat) meio-passado(a)
to meet *(by chance)* encontrar
  (by arrangement) encontrar-se com
  pleased to meet you prazer em conhecê-lo(a)
meeting a reunião
melon o melão
to melt fundir ; derreter
member *(of club, etc)* o sócio
men os homens
to mend arranjar
meningitis a meningite
menu a ementa

set menu a ementa fixa
meringue o merengue
message a mensagem
meter o contador
metre o metro
microwave oven o micro-ondas
midday o meio-dia
midnight a meia-noite
  at midnight à meia-noite
migraine a enxaqueca
  I've a migraine tenho uma enxaqueca
mile a milha
milk o leite
  fresh milk o leite fresco
  hot milk o leite quente
  long-life milk o leite ultrapasteurizado
  powdered milk o leite em pó
  semi-skimmed milk o leite meio-gordo
  skimmed milk o leite magro
  soya milk o leite de soja
  with milk com leite
milkshake o batido de leite
millenium o milénio
millimetre o milímetro
million o milhão
mince *(meat)* a carne picada
mind *n* a mente
mind *vb* ocupar-se de ; objectar
  do you mind if ...? importa-se?
  I don't mind não me importo
mineral water a água mineral
minimum o mínimo
minister *(political)* o ministro
  (church) o pastor
mink o vison
mint *(herb)* a hortelã
  (sweet) o rebuçado de mentol
minute o minuto
mirror o espelho
to miss *(plane, train, etc)* perder
Miss... Menina...

missing *(lost)* perdido(a)
  my son is missing o meu filho desapareceu
mistake o erro
misty: *it's misty* há nevoeiro
misunderstanding o mal-entendido
to mix misturar
mixer a batedeira
mobile phone o telemóvel
modem o modem
modern moderno(a)
moisturizer o creme hidratante
mole *(on skin)* o sinal
moment: *just a moment* um momento
monastery o mosteiro
Monday Segunda-feira
money o dinheiro
  I've no money não tenho dinheiro nenhum
money order o vale postal
monkey o macaco
month o mês
  this month este mês
  last month o mês passado
  next month o mês que vem
monthly mensalmente
monument o monumento
moon a lua
mooring o atracadouro
mop a esfregona
moped a motocicleta
more mais
  more than 3 mais de três
  more bread mais pão
morning a manhã
  in the morning de manhã
  this morning esta manhã
  tomorrow morning amanhã de manhã
mosque a mesquita
mosquito o mosquito

m

m

mosquito net o mosquiteiro
most: most of a maioria de
moth (clothes) a traça
mother a mãe
mother-in-law a sogra
motor o motor
motorbike a moto
motorboat o barco a motor
motorcycle a motocicleta
motorway a auto-estrada
mountain a montanha
mountain bike a bicicleta de montanha
mountain rescue o socorro para alpinistas
mountaineering alpinismo
mouse o rato
mousse (food) a mousse (hair) a espuma
moustache o bigode
mouth a boca
mouthwash desinfectante para a boca
Mr Senhor
Mrs Senhora
Ms Senhora
much muito(a)
  too much demais
mud a lama
mugging o assalto
mumps a papeira
muscle o músculo
museum o museu
mushroom o cogumelo
music a música
musical o musical
mussel o mexilhão
must (to have to) dever
mustard a mostarda
mutton o carneiro
my meu (minha)

N

nail (metal) o prego (on finger) a unha
nailbrush a escova das unhas
nail clippers o corta-unhas
nail file a lima para as unhas
nail polish o verniz das unhas
nail polish remover a acetona
nail scissors as tesouras para as unhas
name o nome
  my name is... o meu nome é...
  what's your name? como é que te chamas?
nanny a ama
napkin o guardanapo
nappy a fralda
narrow estreito(a)
national nacional
national park o parque nacional
nationality a nacionalidade
nature a natureza
navy blue azul-marinho
near to perto
  near to the bank perto do banco
  is it near? fica perto?
necessary necessário(a)
neck o pescoço
necklace o colar
nectarine a nectarina
to need precisar de
  I need... preciso de
  we need... precisamos de
  I need to go tenho que ir
needle a agulha
  a needle and thread uma agulha e a linha
negative (photo) a película
neighbour o/a vizinho(a)
nephew o sobrinho
nest o ninho

net a rede
nettle a urtiga
never nunca
  I never drink wine nunca bebo vinho
new novo(a)
news a notícia
newsagent a tabacaria
newspaper o jornal
newsstand o quiosque
New Year o Ano Novo
  happy New Year! Feliz Ano Novo!
New Year's Eve a véspera de Ano Novo
New Zealand a Nova Zelândia
next próximo(a)
  next to ao lado de
  next week a semana que vem
  the next stop a próxima paragem
  the next train o próximo comboio
nice *(person, holiday)* agradável *(place)* bonito(a)
niece a sobrinha
night a noite
  at night à noite
  last night ontem à noite
  per night por noite
  tomorrow night amanhã à noite
  tonight hoje à noite
night club a boite
nightdress a camisa de noite
no não
  no entry entrada proibida
  no smoking proibido fumar *(without)* sem
  no sugar sem açúcar
  no ice sem gelo
nobody ninguém
noise o barulho
noisy barulhento(a)
  it's very noisy há muito barulho

nonalcoholic não-alcoólico(a)
none nenhum(a)
  there's none left não sobrou nada
non-smoking não-fumador
north o norte
Northern Ireland a Irlanda do Norte
North Sea o Mar do Norte
nose o nariz
not não
  I don't know não sei
note a nota
note pad o bloco-notas
nothing nada
notice o aviso
notice board o placar
novel o romance
November Novembro
now agora
nuclear nuclear
nudist beach a praia para nudistas
number o número
numberplate *(car)* a matrícula
nurse o/a enfermeiro(a)
nut *(to eat)* a noz *(for bolt)* a porca
nutmeg a noz moscada

O

oak o carvalho
oar o remo
oats a aveia
to obtain obter
obvious óbvio(a)
occasionally às vezes
occupation *(work)* a ocupação
ocean o oceano
October Outubro
octopus o polvo
odd *(number)* ímpar

of de
  a glass of wine um copo de vinho
  made of... feito de...
off *(radio, engine, etc)* desligado(a)
  (milk, food, etc) estragado(a)
offer oferecer
office o escritório
often muitas vezes
oil o óleo
oil filter o filtro do óleo
oil gauge o indicador do óleo
ointment a pomada
OK está bem
old velho(a)
  how old are you? que idade
  tem?
  I'm ... years old tenho ... anos
old age pensioner o/a reforma-
do(a)
olive a azeitona
olive oil o azeite
omelette a omeleta
on *(light, TV)* aceso(a)
  (engine) a trabalhar
on em
  on the table na mesa
  on time a horas
once uma vez
  at once imediatamente
one um (uma)
one-way de sentido único
onion a cebola
only somente
open *adj* aberto(a)
to open abrir
opera a ópera
operation *(surgical)* a operação
operator *(phone)* o/a telefonista
opposite (to) em frente de
optician's o oculista
or ou
  tea or coffee chá ou café
orange *adj* cor-de-laranja

orange *(fruit)* a laranja
  (colour) cor-de-laranja
orange juice o sumo de laranja
order: out of order fora de serviço
to order *(in restaurant)* pedir
  can I order? posso pedir?
oregano o orégão
organic biológico(a)
to organize organizar
other: the other one o/a outro(a)
  have you any others? tem
  outros(as)?
original original
ounce = approx. 30 g
our nosso(a)
out *(light)* fora
  he's gone out ele saiu
out of order fora de serviço
outdoor ao ar livre
outside: it's outside está lá fora
oven o forno
oven gloves as luvas de cozinhas
ovenproof refratário(a)
over *(on top of)* sobre
to be overbooked ter mais reser-
vas que lugares
to overcharge cobrar demais
overcoat o sobretudo
overdone *(food)* cozido demais
overdose a dose excessiva
to overheat aquecer demasiado
to overload sobrecarregar
to overtake *(in car)* ultrapassar
to owe dever
  you owe me... deve-me...
  I owe you... devo-lhe
owl o mocho
owner o/a dono(a)
oxygen o oxigénio
oyster a ostra

P

pacemaker o pacemaker
to pack bags fazer as malas
package o embrulho
package tour a viagem organizada
packet o pacote
padded envelope o envelope almofadado
paddling pool a piscina para crianças
padlock o cadeado
paid pago(a)
 I've paid já paguei
pain a dor
painful doloroso(a)
painkiller o analgésico
to paint pintar
paintbrush o pincel
painting a pintura ; o quadro
pair o par
palace o palácio
pale pálido
pan *(frying)* a frigideira
 (saucepan) o tacho
pancake a panqueca
panniers *(for bike)* as bolsas para a bicicleta
pants *(briefs)* as cuecas
paper o papel
paper napkins os guardanapos de papel
papoose *(for carrying baby)* a mochila para levar o bebé
paracetomol® o paracetamol
paraffin o óleo de parafina
parcel a encomenda
pardon desculpe?
 I beg your pardon! desculpe-me!
parents os pais
park o parque
to park estacionar

parking disk o disco de estacionamento
parking meter o parquímetro
parking ticket a multa por estacionamento em lugar proibido
parsley a salsa
parsnip a cenoura branca
part a parte
partner *(business)* o/a sócio(a)
 (friend) o/a companheiro(a)
party *(celebration)* a festa
 (political) o partido
pass *(mountain)* o desfiladeiro
 (train, bus) o passe
passenger o/a passageiro(a)
passport o passaporte
passport control o controle de passaportes
pasta as massas
pastry *(dough)* a massa
 (cake) o bolo
pâté o paté
path o caminho
pavement o passeio
to pay pagar
 I'd like to pay quero pagar
 where do I pay? onde é que se paga?
payment o pagamento
payphone o telefone público
peace a paz
peach o pêssego
peak rate a taxa alta
peanut o amendoim
peanut butter a manteiga de amendoim
pear a pêra
pearls as pérolas
peas as ervilhas
pedal o pedal
pedestrian o/a peão
pedestrian crossing a passadeira para peões

p

to peel *(fruit)* descascar
peg *(clothes)* a mola
 (tent) a estaca
pen a caneta
pencil o lápis
penfriend o/a correspondente
penicillin a penicilina
penis o pénis
penknife o canivete
pensioner o/a reformado(a)
pepper *(spice)* a pimenta
 (vegetable) o pimento
per
 per day por dia
 per hour por hora
 per week por semana
 per person por pessoa
 50 km per hour 50 km por hora
perch *(fish)* a perca
perfect perfeito(a)
performance a representação
 the next performance a próxima representação
perfume o perfume
perhaps talvez
period *(menstruation)* a menstruação
perm a permanente
permit a licença
person a pessoa
 per person por pessoa
personal organizer a agenda
personal stereo o Walkman®
pet o animal doméstico
petrol a gasolina
 4 star petrol a gasolina super
 unleaded petrol a gasolina sem chumbo
petrol cap a tampa do depósito de gasolina

p

petrol pump a bomba de gasolina
petrol station a estação de serviço

petrol tank o depósito da gasolina
pewter o estanho
pharmacy a farmácia
pheasant o faisão
phone see telephone
phonecard o credifone
photocopy a fotocópia
photograph a fotografia
 to take a photograph tirar uma fotografia
phrase book o guia de conversação
piano o piano
pickled de conserva
pickpocket o/a carteirista
picnic o piquenique
 to have a picnic fazer um piquenique
picnic area a zona de piqueniques
picnic rug a manta
picture *(on wall)* o quadro
pie *(savoury)* a empada
 (sweet) a torta
piece o bocado
pier o cais
pill o comprimido
 to be on the Pill tomar a pílula
pillow a almofada
pillowcase a fronha
pin o alfinete
 safety pin o alfinete de segurança
pineapple o ananás
pink cor-de-rosa
pint = approx. 0.5 litre
 a pint of beer uma caneca de cerveja
pipe *(for smoking)* o cachimbo
 (drain, etc) o tubo ; o cano
place o lugar
plain *(yoghurt, etc)* natural

plane o avião
plaster *(sticking)* o adesivo
  (for broken limb) o gesso
plastic o plástico
plate o prato
platform *(railway)* a plataforma
  which platform? qual é a
  plataforma?
play *(at theatre)* a peça
to play jogar
playroom o quarto de brinquedos
pleasant agradável
please por favor
please por favor
  pleased to meet you prazer em
  conhecê-lo(a)
pliers o alicate
plug *(electric)* a ficha ; a tomada
  (for sink) a válvula
plum a ameixa
plumber o canalizador
plunger *(for sink)* o desentupidor
poached *(fish)* cozido(a)
  poached egg ovo escalfado
points *(in car)* os platinados
poison veneno
poisonous venenoso(a)
police *(force)* a polícia
police officer o/a polícia
police station a esquadra
polish *(for shoes)* a pomada para o
  calçado
  (for furniture) a cera
polluted poluído(a)
pollution a poluição
pony trekking o passeio a cavalo
pool a piscina
poor pobre
poorly: he feels poorly ele não
  se sente bem
poppy a papoila
pop socks as meias até o joelho
popular popular

pork a carne de porco
port *(wine)* o vinho do porto
  (seaport) o porto
porter *(for door)* o porteiro
  (for luggage) o carregador
Portugal Portugal
Portuguese português
  (portuguesa)
  (language) o português
possible possível
post: by post pelo correio
postbox o marco do correio
postcard o postal
postcode o código postal
postman/woman o/a carteiro/a
post office os correios
to postpone adiar
pot *(for cooking)* a panela
potato a batata
  baked potato a batata assada
  boiled potatoes as batatas cozidas
  fried potatoes as batatas fritas
  mashed potatoes o puré de
  batata
  roast potatoes as batatas
  assadas
  sauteed potatoes as batatas
  salteadas
potato masher o passe-vite
potato peeler o descascador de
  batatas
potato salad a salada de batata
pothole o buraco
pottery a cerâmica
pound *(money)* a libra
  (weight) = approx. 0.5 kilo
to pour deitar
powder: *in powdered form* em pó
powdered milk o leite em pó
pram o carrinho do bebé
prawn o lagostim
to pray rezar

p
p
p

p

prayer a oração
to prefer preferir
pregnant grávida
   I'm pregnant estou grávida
to prepare preparar
to prescribe receitar
prescription a receita médica
present *(gift)* o presente
press *(newspapers)* a imprensa
pressure pressão
   blood pressure a tensão arterial
pretty bonito(a)
price o preço
price list a lista de preços
priest o padre
prince o príncipe
princess a princesa
print *(photo)* a cópia
private privado(a)
prize o prémio
probably provavelmente

p

problem o problema
programme o programa
professor o/a profesor(a) catedrático(a)
prohibited proibido(a)
to promise prometer
pronounce pronunciar
   how is this pronounced? como se pronuncia isto?
Protestant protestante
prune a ameixa seca
public público(a)
public holiday o feriado
publisher o/a editor(a)
pudding o pudim
to pull puxar
   I've pulled a muscle distendi o músculo

p

pullover o pulover
pump a bomba
pumpkin a abóbora
puncture o furo

puppet o fantoche
puppet show o teatro de marionetes; os fantoches
puppy o cachorro
purple roxo(a)
purpose: *on purpose* de propósito
purse o porta-moedas
to push empurrar
pushchair o carrinho
to put pôr
pyjamas o pijama

Q

quail a codorniz
quality a qualidade
quantity a quantidade
quarantine a quarentena
to quarrel discutir
quarter o quarto
quay o cais
queen a rainha
question a pergunta
queue a fila ; a bicha
to queue fazer fila
quick rápido(a)
quickly depressa
quiet *(place)* sossegado(a)
quilt o edredão
quite: *it's quite good* é bastante bom
   it's quite expensive é muito caro
quiz o concurso

R

rabbit o coelho
rabies a raiva
race *(sport)* a corrida
   (human) a raça*

race course o hipódromo
rack *(luggage)* o porta-bagagens
racket a raqueta
radiator o radiador
radio o rádio
radish o rabanete
raffle a rifa
rag o trapo
railway o caminho-de-ferro
railway station a estação de comboio
rain a chuva
to rain: *it's raining* está a chover
rainbow o arco-íris
raincoat o impermeável
raining: *it's raining* está a chover
raisin a passa de uva
rake o ancinho
rape a violação
to rape violar
rare *(unique)* raro(a)
  (steak) mal passado(a)
rash *(skin)* a urticária
raspberries a framboesa
rat o rato
rate *(price)* a taxa
rate of exchange o câmbio
raw cru(a)
razor a máquina de barbear
razor blades as lâminas de barbear
to read ler
ready pronto(a)
  to get ready preparar-se
real real
rearview mirror o retrovisor
reason a razão
receipt o recibo
receiver *(phone)* o auscultador
recently recentemente
reception (desk) a recepção
receptionist o/a recepcionista
to recharge recarregar

recipe a receita
to recognize reconhecer
to recommend recomendar
record *(music)* o disco
to recover *(from illness)* recuperar
red vermelho(a)
redcurrants as groselhas
to reduce reduzir
reduction o desconto
reel *(fishing)* o carretel
referee o/a árbitro
refill a recarga
refund o reembolso
to refuse recusar
region a região
to register *(at hotel)* preencher o registro
registered *(letter)* registado(a)
registration form a folha de registo
regulations os regulamentos
to reimburse reembolsar
relation *(family)* o parente
to relax repousar
reliable de confiança
to remain ficar
to remember lembrar-se de
  I don't remember não me lembro
remote control o controlo à distância
rent a renda
to rent alugar
rental o aluguer
to repair reparar
to repeat repetir
to reply responder
report o relatório
to request pedir
to require precisar de
to rescue salvar
reservation a reserva

r

to **reserve** reservar
reserved reservado(a)
resident (at hotel) o/a hóspede
resort a estância
rest (repose) o descanso
(remainder) o resto
the rest of the wine o resto do
vinho
to **rest** descansar
restaurant o restaurante
restaurant car o vagão
restaurante
to **retire** reformar-se
retired reformado(a)
to **return** (to go back) voltar
(to give something back) devolver
return ticket o bilhete de ida e
volta
to **reverse** fazer marcha atrás
reverse-charge call a chamada
pagável no destino
reverse gear a marcha atrás
rheumatism o reumatismo
rhubarb o ruibarbo
ribbon a fita
rice o arroz
rich (person) rico(a)
(food) suculento(a)
to **ride** (horse) montar a cavalo
right (correct) certo(a)
to be right ter razão
right: *on/to the right* à direita
ring (for finger) o anel
ring road a circunvalação
ripe maduro(a)
river o rio
road a estrada
road map o mapa das estradas
road sign o sinal de trânsito
roadworks as obras na estrada
roast assado(a)
robber o ladrão
robin o pintarroxo

roll (bread) o pãozinho
rollerblades os patins em linha
rolling pin o rolo da massa
romance (novel) o romance
Romanesque românico(a)
romantic romântico(a)
roof o telhado
roof rack o tejadilho
room (in house, hotel) o quarto
(space) espaço
double room o quarto de casal
single room o quarto individual
room number o número do quarto
room service o serviço de quarto
root a raiz
rope a corda
rosé o vinho rosé
rosemary o alecrim
rosé wine o vinho rosé
rotten (fruit, etc) podre ;
estragado(a)
rough (surface) áspero(a)
(sea) agitado(a)
round (shape) redondo(a)
roundabout (traffic) a rotunda
route a rota
row (line) a fila
to **row** (boat) remar
rowing (sport) o remo
rowing boat o barco a remos
royal real
rubber a borracha
rubber band o elástico
rubber gloves as luvas de
borracha
rubbish o lixo
rubella a rubéola
rucksack a mochila
rudder o leme
rug o tapete
ruins as ruínas
ruler (for measuring) a régua

rum o rum
to run correr
rush hour a hora de ponta
rusty ferrugento(a)
rye o centeio

S

saccharin a sacarina
sad triste
saddle *(bike)* o selim
 (horse) a sela
safe *(for valuables)* o cofre
safe seguro(a)
 is it safe? é seguro?
safety belt o cinto de segurança
safety pin o alfinete de segurança
sage *(herb)* a salva
to sail *(sport, leisure)* velejar
sail(ing) a vela
sailboard a prancha
sailing boat barco à vela
saint santo(a)
salad a salada
 green salad a salada verde
 mixed salad a salada mista
 potato salad a salada de
 batatas
 tomato salad a salada de
 tomate
salad dressing o tempero da
 salada
salami o salame
sale(s) o saldo
salesman/woman o/a vendedor(a)
sales rep o/a representante de
 vendas
salmon o salmão
 smoked salmon o salmão fumado
salt o sal
salt water a água salgada
salty salgado(a)
same mesmo(a)

sample a amostra
sand a areia
sandals as sandálias
sandwich a sandes
 toasted sandwich a tosta
sanitary towel o penso higiénico
sardine a sardinha
satellite dish a antena parabólica
satellite TV a televisão via
 satélite
Saturday o sábado
sauce o molho
 tomato sauce molho de tomate
saucepan a caçarola
saucer o pires
sauna a sauna
sausage a salsicha
to save *(life)* salvar
 (money) poupar
savoury saboroso(a)
savouries os salgados
saw a serra
to say dizer
scales *(weighing)* a balança
scallops as vieiras
scampi as gambas panadas
scarf *(woollen)* o cachecol
 (headscarf) o lenço (de pescoço)
school a escola
scissors a tesoura
score *(of match)* o resultado
to score marcar
Scotland a Escócia
Scottish escocês (escocesa)
scouring pad o esfregão Bravo®
screen *(computer, TV)* o ecrã
screenwash o detergente para o
 pára-brisas
screw o parafuso
screwdriver a chave de parafusos
 phillips screwdriver® o
 phillips®
scuba diving o mergulho

S

sculpture a escultura
sea o mar
seafood o peixe e o marisco
seagull a gaivota
seal a foca
seasick enjoado(a)
  I get seasick enjoo
seaside a praia
  at the seaside na praia
season *(of year)* a estação
  in season da época
season ticket o passe
seasoning o tempero
seat *(chair)* a cadeira
  (on bus, train, etc) o lugar
seatbelt o cinto de segurança
seaweed a alga marinha
second segundo(a)
second class de segunda classe
second-hand em segunda mão ;
  usado(a)

S

secretary o/a secretário(a)
security guard o segurança
to see ver
seed a semente
self-catering com cozinha
self-employed que trabalha por
  conta própria
self-service o auto-serviço
to sell vender
  do you sell...? tem...?
Sellotape ® a fita-cola
semi-skimmed milk leite meio-
  gordo
to send mandar
senior citizen o/a reformado(a)
separated separado(a)
separately: *to pay separately*
  pagar separadamente

S

September Setembro
septic tank a fossa séptica
sequel *(film, book)* a continuação
serious grave ; sério(a)

to serve servir
service o serviço
service charge o custo do serviço
serviette o guardanapo
set menu a refeição a preço fixo
several vários(as)
to sew coser
sex o sexo
shade a sombra
shallow pouco profundo(a)
shampoo o champô
shampoo and set a lavagem e mise
to share repartir ; dividir
sharp *(razor, knife)* afiado(a)
to shave fazer a barba
shaving cream o creme de barbear
shawl o xaile
she ela *see* **GRAMMAR**
sheep a ovelha
sheet *(for bed)* o lençol
shelf a prateleira
shell *(seashell)* a concha
  (egg, nut) a casca
shellfish o marisco
sheltered abrigado(a)
shepherd o pastor
sherry o xerez
to shine brilhar
shingles *(illness)* o herpes zóster
ship o barco
shirt a camisa
shock absorber o amortecedor
shoe o sapato
shoe mender's o sapateiro
shoe polish a graxa
shoe shop a sapataria
shop a loja
shop assistant o/a vendedor(a)
shopping: *go shopping* ir às
  compras
shopping centre o centro comercial

shore a costa
short curto(a)
short cut o atalho
shorts os calções
short-sighted míope
shoulder o ombro
to shout gritar
show o espectáculo
to show mostrar
shower o duche
  to take a shower tomar um duche
  (rain) o chuveiro ; o aguaceiro
shower cap a touca
shower curtain a cortina do chuveiro
shrimps os camarões
to shrink encolher
shut *(closed)* fechado(a)
to shut fechar
shutters as persianas ; as gelosias
shy tímido(a)
sick *(ill)* doente
  I feel sick sinto-me mal-disposto(a)
side dish o acompanhamento
sidelight o farolim
sidewalk o passeio
sieve *(for liquids)* o coador
  (for flour) a peneira
to sightsee fazer turismo
sightseeing o turismo
sign *(road-, notice, etc)* o sinal ; a sinalização
to sign assinar
signature a assinatura
silk a seda
silver a prata
similar similar
simple simples
to sing cantar
single *(not married)* solteiro(a)
single bed a cama de pessoa só

single room o quarto individual
sink o lava-louça
sir senhor
sister a irmã
to sit sentar-se
size *(clothes)* o tamanho
  (shoes) o número
to skate patinar
skates os patins
skating ring o rinque de patinagem
ski o esqui
to ski esquiar
skimmed milk leite magro
skin a pele
skindiving o mergulho
skirt a saia
sky o céu
slang o calão
sledge o trenó
to sleep dormir
sleeper *(on train)* a carruagem-cama
sleeping bag o saco cama
sleeping pill o comprimido para dormir
slice a fatia
slide *(photograph)* o diapositivo
to slip escorregar
slippers os chinelos
slow lento(a)
small pequeno(a)
smaller mais pequeno(a)
smell o cheiro
smile o sorriso
to smile sorrir
smoke o fumo
to smoke fumar
  I don't smoke não fumo
smoke alarm o alarme contra incêndios
smoked fumado(a)
smokers os fumadores

139

S

smooth liso(a) ; macio(a)
snack o lanche
 to have a snack comer qualquer
 coisa
snack bar o snack-bar
snake a cobra
snake bite a mordedura de cobra
to sneeze espirrar
to snore ressonar
snorkel o tubo de ar
snow a neve
to snow nevar
snowboard o snowboard
snow chains as correntes para a
 neve
snowman o boneco-de-neve
so portanto
 so much tanto(a)
soap o sabão ; o sabonete
soap powder o sabão em pó
sober sóbrio(a)
socket *(electrical)* a tomada
socks as peúgas
soda water água com gás
sofa o sofá
sofa bed o sofá-cama
soft macio(a)
soft drink o refrigerante
software o software
soldier o soldado
sole *(fish)* o linguado
 (of shoe) a sola
soluble solúvel
some alguns (algumas)
someone alguém
something alguma coisa
sometimes às vezes
son o filho
son-in-law o genro
song a canção
soon em breve
 as soon as possible o antes
 possível

sore magoado(a)
sore throat: *I have sore throat*
 dói-me a garganta
sorry: *I'm sorry!* lamento
sort: *what sort of cheese?* que
 tipo de queijo?
sound o som
soup a sopa
sour azedo(a)
soured cream as natas azedas
south o sul
souvenir a recordação
spa as termas
space o espaço
spade a enxada
Spain a Espanha
Spanish espanhol(a)
 (language) o espanhol
spanner a chave inglesa
spare parts as peças sobresse-
 lentes
spare wheel a roda sobressalente
sparkling espumoso(a)
 sparkling water água com gás
 sparkling wine o espumante
spark plug a vela
to speak falar
special especial
speciality a especialidade
speed a velocidade
speed limit o limite de velocidade
speedometer o conta-quilómet-
 ros
spell: *how do you spell it?* como
 se escreve?
to spend *(money)* gastar
spices as especiarias
spicy picante
spider a aranha
to spill entornar
spinach o espinafre
spine a coluna
spirits as bebidas espirituosas

splinter a falha, a lasca
spoke *(wheel)* o raio
sponge a esponja
spoon a colher
sport o desporto
spring *(season)* a primavera
spring onion a cebolinha
square *(in town)* a praça
squash *(drink)* o sumo
  (game) o squash
to squeeze apertar
squid as lulas
stadium o estádio
stain a nódoa
stained glass o vitral
stairs a escada
stale *(bread)* duro(a)
stalls *(in theatre)* a plateia
stamp *(postage)* o selo
star *(in sky, in films)* a estrela
to start começar
starter *(in meal)* a entrada
  (in car) o motor de arranque
station a estação
stationer's a papelaria
to stay ficar
  I'm staying at a hotel fico num hotel
steak o bife
  medium steak o bife ao ponto
  well-done steak o bife bem-passado
  rare steak o bife mal-passado
to steal roubar
steamed cozido(a) a vapor
steel aço
steep: is it steep? custa a subir?
steeple o campanário
steering wheel o volante
stepfather o padrasto
stepmother a madrasta
stereo o estéreo
  personal stereo o Walkman®

sterling *(pounds)* esterlino(a)
stew o guisado
steward *(on plane)* o comissário de bordo
stewardess *(on plane)* a hospedeira de bordo
to stick *(with glue)* colar
sticking plaster o adesivo
still *(not moving)* imóvel
  (not sparkling) sem gás
sting a picada
to sting picar
stitches *(surgical)* os pontos
stock cube o cubo de caldo
stockings as meias
stomach o estômago
stomach upset o mal-estar de estômago
stone a pedra
  (measurement) = approx. 6.5 kg
to stop parar
store *(shop)* a loja
storey o andar
storm a tempestade
story a história
straightaway imediatamente
straight on sempre em frente
strainer o coador
straw *(for drinking)* a palha
strawberry o morango
stream o riacho
street a rua
street map o mapa das ruas
stress o stress
strike *(of workers)* a greve
string o cordel ; o fio
striped às riscas
stroke *(medical)* a trombose
strong forte
stuck: it's stuck está preso(a)
student o/a estudante
stuffed recheado(a)

S

stung picado(a)
stupid estúpido(a)
subscription a assinatura
subtitles as legendas
suddenly de repente
suede a camurça
sugar o açúcar
  icing sugar o açúcar em pó
sugar-free sem açúcar
suit *(men's and women's)* o fato
suitcase a mala
summer o verão
summer holidays as férias de
  Verão
sun o sol
to sunbathe tomar banhos de sol
sunblock o protector solar
sunburn a queimadura de sol
Sunday o domingo
sunflower o girassol
sunflower oil o óleo de girassol
sunglasses os óculos de sol
sunny: *it's sunny* está sol
sunrise o nascer do sol ; o ama-
  nhecer
sunroof o tecto de abrir
sunscreen o filtro solar
sunset o pôr do sol ; o ocaso
sunshade o guarda-sol ; a sombra
sunstroke a insolação
suntan o bronzeado
suntan lotion a loção de
  bronzear
supermarket o supermercado
supper a ceia
supplement o suplemento
surcharge a sobretaxa
sure seguro(a)
surfboard a prancha de surf
surgery *(operation)* a cirurgia
  (building) o consultório
surname o apelido

surprise a surpresa
surrounded by rodeado(a) por
to swallow engolir
swan o cisne
to sweat suar
sweater o pulover
sweatshirt a sweatshirt
sweet *(not savoury)* doce
sweet *(dessert)* a sobremesa
sweetener o edulcorante
sweets os doces ; as guloseimas
to swell *(injury etc)* inchar
to swim nadar
swimming pool a piscina
swimsuit o fato de banho
swing *(for children)* o baloiço
Swiss suíço(a)
switch o interruptor
to switch off apagar ; desligar
to switch on acender ; ligar
Switzerland a Suíça
swollen *(finger, ankle, etc)* inchado(a)
swordfish o espadarte
synagogue a sinagoga
syringe a seringa

T

table a mesa
tablecloth a toalha de mesa
tablespoon a colher de sopa
tablet *(pill)* o comprimido
table tennis o ping-pong
tail o rabo, a cauda
tailor's a alfaiataria
take *(medicine etc)* tomar
  how long does it take? quanto
  tempo demora?
take-away *(food)* para levar
to take off levantar voo
to take out *(of bag etc)* tirar
talc o talco

to talk to conversar
tall alto(a)
tame *(animal)* manso(a)
tampons os tampões
tangerine a tangerina
tank o tanque
tap a torneira
tape *(video)* a cassette de vídeo
tape measure a fita métrica
tape recorder o gravador
tarragon o estragão
tart a tarte
tartar sauce o molho tártaro
taste o sabor
to taste provar
  can I taste it? posso provar?
tax o imposto
taxi o táxi
taxi driver o/a taxista
taxi rank a praça de táxis
tea o chá
  herbal tea a tisana
  lemon tea chá de limão
  strong tea chá forte
teabag o saquinho de chá
to teach ensinar
teacher o/a professor(a)
team a equipa
teapot o bule
tear *(in eye)* a lágrima
  (in material) o rasgão
teaspoon a colher de chá
teat *(on baby's bottle)* a tetina
tea towel o pano de cozinha
teeshirt a camisola de manga
  curta
teeth os dentes
telegram o telegrama
telephone o telefone
  mobile telephone o telemóvel
to telephone telefonar
telephone box a cabine telefónica
telephone call a chamada

telephone card o cartão telefónico
telephone directory a lista telefónica
telephone number o número de telefone
television a televisão
television set o televisor
telex o telex
to tell dizer
temperature a temperatura
  to have a temperature ter febre
temple o templo
temporary temporário(a)
tendon o tendão
tennis o ténis
tennis ball a bola de ténis
tennis court o campo de ténis
tennis racket a raqueta de ténis
tent a tenda
tent peg a estaca
terminal *(airport)* o terminal
terrace a esplanada
terracotta a terracota
terrorist o/a terrorista
than que
  better than melhor do que
  more than you mais do que tu
  more than five mais de cinco
to thank agradecer
thank you obrigado(a)
  thank you very much muito obrigado(a)
that aquele (aquela)
that one esse (essa)
theatre o teatro
theft o roubo
their seu (sua)
then então
there *(over there)* ali
there is/there are há
thermometer o termómetro
these estes (estas)
  these ones estes (estas)

they eles (elas) see GRAMMAR
thick grosso(a)
thief o ladrão
thigh a coxa
thin *(person)* magro(a)
thing a coisa
  my things as minhas coisas
to think pensar
  (to be of opinion) achar
third terceiro(a)
thirsty: *I'm thirsty* tenho sede
this este (esta)
this one este (esta)
thorn o espinho
those aqueles (aquelas)
those ones aqueles (aquelas)
thousand mil
thread a linha
thriller *(film)* o filme de suspense
  (book) o livro de suspense
throat a garganta
throat lozenges as pastilhas para
  a garganta
through através de
thrush *(candida)* a candidíase
  vaginal
thumb o polegar
thunder o trovão
thunderstorm o temporal
Thursday a quinta-feira
thyme o tomilho
ticket o bilhete
  a single ticket o bilhete de ida
  a return ticket o bilhete de ida
  e volta
  a tourist ticket o bilhete de
  turista
  a book of tickets a caderneta
  de bilhetes
ticket collector o revisor
ticket office a bilheteira
tide *(sea)* a maré
  low tide a maré baixa

  high tide a maré alta
tie a gravata
tight apertado(a)
tights os collants
till *(cash desk)* a caixa
till *(until)* até
  till 2 o'clock até ás duas
time o tempo
  (clock) as horas
  what time is it? que horas são?
  this time esta vez
timetable o horário
tin *(can)* a lata
tinfoil a folha de alumínio
tin-opener o abre-latas
tip a gorjeta
to tip dar uma gorjeta
tipped *(cigarette)* com filtro
Tippex® o fluido corrector
tired cansado(a)
tissues o lenço de papel
to a
  to London para Londres
  to the airport ao aeroporto
toast *(to eat)* a torrada
  (raising glass) brindar
tobacco o tabaco
tobacconist's a tabacaria
today hoje
toe o dedo
together juntos
toilet a casa de banho
  toilets for disabled a casa de
  banho para deficientes
toilet brush a escova da sanita
toilet paper o papel higiénico
toiletries os artigos de toilette
token *(for bus)* o bilhete, a senha
toll *(motorway)* a portagem
tomato o tomate
tomato juice o sumo de tomate
tomato purée o concentrado de
  tomate

tomato sauce o molho de tomate
tomato soup a sopa de tomate
tomorrow amanhã
  tomorrow morning amanhã de manhã
  tomorrow afternoon amanhã à tarde
  tomorrow evening amanhã ao fim da tarde/à noite
tongue a língua
tonic water a água tónica
tonight esta noite
tonsillitis a amigdalite
too *(also)* também
  too big grande demais
  too small pequeno(a) demais
  too hot (food) quente demais
  too noisy demasiado barulhento(a)
tool a ferramenta
toolkit o jogo de ferramentas
tooth o dente
toothache a dor de dentes
toothbrush a escova de dentes
toothpaste a pasta dentífrica
top: *the top floor* o último andar
top *(of hill)* a parte de cima
  on top of ... em cima de...
topless: *to go topless* fazer topless
torch *(flashlight)* a lanterna
torn rasgado(a)
total *(amount)* o total
to touch tocar
tough *(meat)* duro(a)
tour *(trip)* a excursão
  (of museum etc) a visita
  guided tour a visita guiada
tour guide o/a guia turístico(a)
tourist o/a turista
tourist office o turismo
tourist route a rota turística
tourist ticket o bilhete turístico

to tow rebocar
towel o toalha
tower a torre
town a cidade
town centre o centro da cidade
town hall a Câmara Municipal
town plan o mapa da cidade
towrope o cabo de reboque
toy o brinquedo
toy shop a loja de brinquedos
tracksuit o fato de treino
traditional tradicional
traffic o trânsito
traffic jam o engarrafamento
traffic lights o semáforo
trailer o reboque
train o comboio
  by train de comboio
  the next train o próximo comboio
  the first train o primeiro comboio
  the last train o último comboio
trainers os sapatos de ténis
tram o eléctrico
tranquillizer o calmante
to translate traduzir
translation a tradução
to travel viajar
travel agent o agente de viagens
travel guide o/a guia turístico(a)
travel sickness enjoo
traveller's cheque o cheque de viagem
tray o tabuleiro ; a bandeja
tree a árvore
trip a viagem
trolley *(luggage, shopping)* o carrinho
trouble os problemas
trousers as calças
trout a truta
truck o camião

t

true verdadeiro(a)
trunk *(luggage)* o baú
trunks *(swimming)* os calções de banho
truth a verdade
to try *(attempt)* tentar
to try on *(clothes, shoes)* provar
T-shirt a T-shirt
Tuesday terça-feira
tulip a túlipa
tuna o atum
tunnel o túnel
turkey o peru
to turn voltar ; girar
to turn off apagar ; desligar *(tap)* fechar
to turn on *(light etc)* acender ; ligar *(tap)* abrir
turnip o nabo

t

turquoise *(colour)* turquesa
tweezers a pinça
twice duas vezes
twin-bedded room o quarto com duas camas
twins gémeos
   identical twins gémeos idênticos
to type escrever à máquina
typical típico
tyre o pneu
tyre pressure a pressão dos pneus

U

ugly feio(a)
ulcer a úlcera
umbrella o guarda-chuva *(sunshade)* o chapéu-de-sol

u

uncle o tio
uncomfortable incómodo(a)
unconscious inconsciente
under debaixo de

underground *(metro)* metropolitano
underpants as cuecas
underpass a passagem subterrânea
understand compreender
   I don't understand não percebo
   do you understand? percebe?
underwear a roupa interior
underwater debaixo da água
undo desfazer
to undress despir-se
unemployed desempregado(a)
to unfasten desapertar ; desabotoar
unhappy with... não estar satisfeito(a) com...
United States os Estados Unidos
university a universidade
unleaded petrol a gasolina sem chumbo
unlucky infeliz
to unpack *(suitcases)* desfazer as malas
to unscrew desaparafusar
up: to get up levantar-se
upside down invertido(a)
upstairs em cima
urgent urgente
urine a urina
USA os EUA
to use utilizar
useful útil
usual habitual
usually geralmente
U-turn a meia-volta

V

vacancies *(in hotel etc)* os quartos vagos
vaccination a vacinação
vacuum cleaner o aspirador

vagina a vagina
valid válido(a)
valley o vale
valuable valioso(a)
valuables os objectos de valor
value o valor
valve a válvula
van a carrinha
vanilla a baunilha
vase *(for flowers)* a jarra
VAT o IVA
veal a carne de vitela
vegan vegetalista
vegetables os legumes
vegetarian vegetariano(a)
  I'm vegetarian sou vegeta-
  riano(a)
vehicle o veículo
vein a veia
Velcro® o Velcro
velvet o veludo
vending machine a máquina de
  venda automática
venereal disease a doença
  venéria
venison a carne de veado
ventilator o ventilador
very muito
vest a camisola interior
vet o/a veterinário(a)
via por
video o vídeo
to video *(from TV)* gravar
video camera a câmara de vídeo
video cassette a videocassete
video game o jogo de vídeo
video phone o videofone
video recorder o gravador de
  video
view a vista
village a aldeia
vinaigrette a vinagreta

vinegar o vinagre
vineyard a vinha
violet *(flower)* a violeta
viper a víbora
virus o vírus
visa o visto
to visit visitar
visiting hours *(hospital)* as horas
  de visita
visitor a visita
vitamin a vitamina
vodka a vodka
voice a voz
volcano o vulcão
volleyball o voleibol
voltage a voltagem
to vomit vomitar
voucher o vale, o recibo

W

wage o salário
waist a cintura
to wait for esperar por
waiter o empregado de mesa
waiting room a sala de espera
waitress a empregada de mesa
to wake up acordar
Wales o País de Gales
to walk andar
walk o passeio
walking boots as botas de montanha
walking stick a bengala
wall *(inside)* a parede
  (outside) o muro
wallet a carteira
walnut a noz
to want querer
war a guerra
wardrobe o guarda-fato
warehouse o armazém

W

warm quente
  it's warm (weather) está calor
warning triangle o triângulo de sinalização
to wash lavar
  to wash oneself lavar-se
washbasin o lavatório
washing machine a máquina de lavar roupa
washing powder o detergente para a roupa
washing-up bowl o lava-louças
washing-up liquid o detergente para a louça
wasp a vespa
waste bin o balde do lixo
watch o relógio
to watch ver, observar
watchstrap a pulseira de relógio
water a água
  cold water a água fria
  drinking water a água potável
  fresh water a água corrente
  hot water a água quente
  salt water a água salgada
  sparkling water a água com gás
  still water a água sem gás
watercress o agrião
waterfall a queda de água
water heater o esquentador
watermelon a melancia
waterproof impermeável
to waterski fazer esqui aquático
water-skiing o esqui aquático
waterwings as braçadeiras
waves as ondas
wax a cera
waxing *(hair removal)* depilação com cera
way a maneira ; o caminho
we nós *see* **GRAMMAR**
weak fraco(a)
  (tea, etc) aguado(a)

to wear vestir
weather o tempo
wedding o casamento
wedding anniversary o aniversário de casamento
wedding cake o bolo de noiva
wedding dress o vestido de noiva
wedding present a prenda de casamento
Wednesday quarta-feira
week a semana
  last week a semana passada
  next week a semana que vem
  per week por semana
  this week esta semana
weekday o dia útil
weekend o fim-de-semana
  next weekend o próximo fim-de-semana
  this weekend este fim-de-semana
weekly por semana
to weigh pesar
weight o peso
welcome bem-vindo(a)
well bem
  he's not well ele não se sente bem
well-done *(steak)* bem-passado
wellington boots as galochas
Welsh galês (galesa)
  (language) o galês
west o oeste
wet molhado(a)
  (weather) chuvoso(a)
wetsuit o fato de mergulhador
what que
  what is it? o que é?
wheel a roda
wheelchair a cadeira de rodas
wheel clamp o imobilizador
when? quando?

where? onde?
which: *which is it?* qual é?
while enquanto
  in a while dentro de pouco
whipped cream o chantilly
whisky o uísque
white branco(a)
who: *who is it?* quem é?
whole inteiro(a)
wholemeal bread o pão integral
whose: *whose is it?* de quem é?
why? porquê?
wide largo(a)
widow a viúva
widower o viúvo
width a largura
wife a mulher ; a esposa
wig a peruca
to win ganhar
wind o vento
windbreak o guarda-vento
windmill o moínho
window a janela
  (shop) a montra
windscreen o pára-brisas
windscreen wipers o limpa-pára-brisas
to windsurf fazer windsurf
windsurfing o wind-surf
windy: *it's windy* está vento
wine o vinho
  red wine o vinho tinto
  white wine o vinho branco
  rosé wine o vinho rosé
  dry wine o vinho seco
  sweet wine o vinho doce
  sparkling wine o vinho espumante
  house wine o vinho da casa
wine list a lista de vinhos
wing mirror o retrovisor exterior
winter o inverno
with com

with ice com gelo
with milk com leite
with sugar com açúcar
without sem
  without ice sem gelo
  without milk sem leite
  without sugar sem açúcar
wolf o lobo
woman a mulher
wood *(substance)* a madeira
woods a floresta
wool a lã
word a palavra
to work *(person)* trabalhar
  (machine) funcionar
  it doesn't work não está a funcionar
world o mundo
worldwide no mundo inteiro
worried preocupado(a)
worse pior
worth: *it's worth...* vale...
to wrap *(parcel, etc)* embrulhar
wrapping paper o papel de embrulho
wrinkles as rugas
wrist o pulso
to write escrever
  please write it down escreve-o, por favor
writing paper o papel de carta
wrong errado(a)
wrought iron o ferro forjado

X

x-ray a radiografia

Y

yacht o iate
year o ano
  last year o ano passado

y

next year o ano que vem
this year este ano
yellow amarelo(a)
Yellow Pages as Páginas
  Amarelas
yes sim
yesterday ontem
yet: *not yet* ainda não
yoghurt o iogurte
  plain yoghurt o iogurte natural
yolk a gema
you você/tu/vocês/vós *see*
  GRAMMAR

young novo(a)
  (person) o/a jovem
your teu (tua)
youth hostel o albergue da
  juventude

Z

zero o zero
zip o fecho éclair
zone a zona
zoo o jardim zoológico

A

a to ; the *(feminine)*
à to the
abadia *f* abbey
abaixo down ; below

ABERTO OPEN

aberto todo o ano open all year round
abrande slow down
abre-garrafas *m* bottle-opener
abre-latas *m* tin/can-opener

ABRIL APRIL

abrir to open; to unlock *(door)*
acabar to end ; to finish
acampar to camp
aceitar to accept
acelerador *m* accelerator
acender to switch/turn on ; to light *(fire, cigarette)*
  acenda as luzes switch on lights
acepipes *mpl* titbits, starters
aceso(a) on *(light, etc)*
acesso *m* access
achar to think ; to find
  acha bem? do you think it's alright?
acidente *m* accident
acima above
aço *m* steel
  aço inoxidável stainless steel
açorda *f* bread porridge/stew
acordo *m* agreement
Açores *mpl* the Azores islands
actual present(-day)
actualizar to modernize ; to update
açúcar *m* sugar

adega *f* wine cellar
adesivo *m* plaster *(for cut)*
adeus goodbye
adiantado(a) fast *(watch)* ; early *(train, etc)*
adulto(a) adult
advogado(a) *m/f* lawyer
aéreo(a): a linha aérea airline
  via aérea air mail
aeroporto *m* airport
agência *f* agency
  agência de viagens travel agents
agente *m/f* agent
agora now

AGOSTO AUGUST

agradável pleasant
agradecer to thank
água *f* water
  água destilada distilled water
  água potável drinking water
aguardente *f* spirit brandy
agudo(a) sharp *(pain)*
ajudar to help
albergue *m* hostel
  albergue da juventude youth hostel
alcoólico(a) alcoholic
aldeia *f* small village
alegre jolly
Alemanha *f* Germany
alérgico(a) a allergic to
alface *f* lettuce
alfaiate *m* tailor

ALFÂNDEGA CUSTOMS

alfinete *m* pin
alforreca *f* jellyfish
algodão *m* cotton
algum(a) some ; any
  alguns (algumas) a few ; some

mais alguma coisa? anything else?

alho *m* garlic

alhos-porros *mpl* leeks

ali there

alimentação *f* food

alívio *m* relief

almoço *m* lunch
   pequeno-almoço breakfast

almofada *f* pillow ; cushion

alojamento *m* accommodation

alpinismo *m* climbing

alto! stop!

alto(a) high ; tall ; loud
   a estação alta high season

altura *f* height

alugar to hire ; to rent

ALUGA-SE TO RENT

   alugam-se quartos rooms to let

aluguer *m* rental

amanhã tomorrow

amarelo(a) yellow

amargo(a) bitter

ambulância *f* ambulance

amêijoa *f* clam ; cockle
   amêijoas à Bulhão Pato clams with coriander, olive oil and garlic

ameixa *f* plum
   ameixa seca prune

amêndoa *f* almond
   amêndoa amarga bitter almond liqueur

amendoim *m* peanut

amigo(a) *m/f* friend

amora *f* blackberry ; mulberry

amortecedor *m* shock absorber

amostra *f* sample

analgésico *m* painkiller

ananás *m* pineapple

anchovas *fpl* anchovies

andar to walk

andar *m* floor ; storey

anel *m* ring

anis *m* aniseed liqueur

aniversário *m* anniversary ; birthday

ano *m* year
   Ano Novo New Year

antes de before

antiguidades *fpl* antiques

apagado(a) off *(radio, etc)* ; out *(light, etc)*

apagar to switch/turn off *(light, etc)*

aparelho *m* gadget ; machine
   aparelho para a surdez hearing aid

apartamento *m* apartment ; flat

apelido *m* surname
   apelido de solteira maiden name

apenas only

apertado(a) tight

apetite *m* appetite
   bom apetite! enjoy your meal!

apólice de seguro *f* insurance certificate

aquecedor *m* heater ; electric fire

aquecimento *m* heating

aqui here

ar *m* air ; choke *(car)*
   ar condicionado air conditioning

arder to burn

areia *f* sand

arenque *m* herring

armário *m* cupboard ; closet

armazém *m* warehouse
   grande armazém department store

arrendar to let

arroz *m* rice
   arroz doce sweet rice dessert

artesanato *m* handicrafts

153

a

artigo m item
  artigos de ménage household goods
  artigos de vime wickerwork
árvore f tree

ASCENSOR LIFT

assado(a) roast ; baked
assinar to sign
assinatura f signature
assistência f audience ; assistance
atacadores mpl laces
até till ; until
aterrar to land
atrás behind
atrasado(a) late (for appointment)
atrasar to delay

ATRASO DELAY

a

atravessar to cross
atum m tuna ; tunny fish
autocarro m bus ; coach
  a paragem de autocarro bus stop

AUTO-ESTRADA MOTORWAY

automobilista m/f driver
automóvel m car
autorização f licence ; permit
avaria f breakdown

AVARIADO OUT OF ORDER

ave f bird
avelã f hazelnut
avenida f avenue
avião m plane
aviso m warning
avô m grandfather
avó f grandmother
azedo(a) sour

azeite m olive oil
azeitona f olive
azul blue
azulejo m ornamental tile

B

bacalhau m salt cod
  bacalhau à Brás salt cod with eggs, onion and potatoes
bagaceira f eau de vie
bagaço m eau de vie
bagagem f luggage ; baggage
Bairrada region producing full-bodied red and aromatic white wines
bairro m quarter ; district
baixar to lower
baixo: em baixo below
balcão m shop counter ; circle in theatre
banco m bank ; seat (in car, etc) ; accident & emergency dept
banheiro m lifeguard
banho m bath
  a casa de banho bathroom
  tomar banho to have a bath
barato(a) cheap
barba f beard
barbeiro m barber
barco m boat ; ship
  barco a remos rowing boat
  barco à vela sailing boat
barraca f hut (shed) ; beach hut
barriga f tummy ; belly
barro m clay pottery ; earthenware
barulho m noise
bastante enough
batata f potato
  batatas fritas chips ; crisps
bater to beat ; to knock

bata à porta please knock
bateria f battery (for car)
batido de leite m milk shake
baunilha f vanilla
bebé m baby
beber to drink
bebida f drink
beco m alley
belo(a) beautiful
bem well
  está bem OK
  bem passado well done (steak)
bem-vindo(a) welcome
bengaleiro m cloakroom (at theatre)
beringela f aubergine
berma f hard shoulder
  bermas baixas steep verge–no hard shoulder
besugo m sea bream
beterraba f beetroot
bica f espresso coffee
bicha f queue
  fazer bicha to queue
bicicleta f bicycle ; cycle
bife m steak
  bife com batatas fritas steak and chips
bifurcação f junction
bilhar m billiards
bilhete m ticket ; fare
  bilhete de entrada admission ticket
  bilhete de identidade identity card

BILHETEIRA TICKET OFFICE

binóculos mpl binoculars
boa see **bom**
boca f mouth
bocado: um bocado a bit ; a portion

boîte f nightclub
bola f ball
  bola de Berlim doughnut
bolacha f biscuit
bolo m cake
  bolo-rei ring-shaped fruit cake eaten at Christmas
bolsa f stock exchange ; handbag
bom (boa) good ; fine (weather) ; kind
  bom dia good morning
  boa noite good evening ; good night
  boa tarde good afternoon
bomba f bomb ; pump (petrol)

BOMBEIROS FIRE BRIGADE

boneco(a) doll ; puppet toy
bonito(a) pretty
borbulha f spot
bordados mpl embroidered items
borrego m lamb
bosque m forest ; woodland
bota f boot (to wear)
braço m arm
branco(a) white
brigada de trânsito f traffic police
brincos mpl earrings
brinquedo m toy
britânico(a) British
broa f corn (maize) bread
  broas corn (maize) cakes
bronzeador m suntan oil
brushing m blow-dry
bugigangas fpl bric-à-brac
buscar to seek
bússola f compass
buzinar to toot car horn

155

C

cabeça *f* head
cabedais *mpl* leather goods
cabeleireiro(a) *m/f* hairdresser
cabelo *m* hair
cabide *m* coat hanger ; peg *(for clothes)*
cabine *f* cabin ; booth
  cabine telefónica phone box
cabo *m* knife handle ; electric lead
  cabos de emergência jump leads
  cabo de reboque tow rope
cabrito *m* kid goat
caça *f* game *(to eat)* ; hunting
cachorro *m* hot dog ; puppy
cada each ; every
cadeado *m* padlock
cadeira *f* chair
  cadeira de bebé high chair ; push chair
  cadeira de lona deck chair
  cadeira de rodas wheelchair
café *m* (black) coffee ; café
cair to fall ; to fall over
cais *m* quay

CAIXA CASH DESK

  caixa automática cash machine
  caixa do correio letterbox
caixote *m* bin
calças *fpl* trousers
calções *mpl* shorts
  calções de banho swimming trunks
calços para travões *mpl* brake pads
caldeirada *f* fish stew
caldo *m* stock *(for soup)*
  caldo verde cabbage soup
calor *m* heat
calorífero *m* heater

cama *f* bed
  cama de casal double bed
  cama de criança cot
  cama de solteiro single bed
  a roupa de cama bedding
câmara de ar *f* inner tube
câmara municipal *f* town hall
camarão *m* shrimp
camarote *m* cabin
cambiar to exchange ; to change money
câmbio *m* exchange rate
camião *m* lorry
caminho *m* path ; way ; route
camioneta *f* coach
camisa *f* shirt
  camisa de noite nightdress
campainha *f* bell *(on door)*
campismo *m* camping
campo *m* field ; countryside
campo de golfe golf course
camurça *f* suede
cancelar to cancel
canela *f* cinnamon
caneta *f* pen
cano de esgoto *m* drain
canoagem *f* canoeing
cansado(a) tired
cantina *f* canteen
canto *m* corner
cão *m* dog
capacete *m* crash helmet
capela *f* chapel
capot *m* bonnet *(of car)*
cara *f* face
caracóis *mpl* snails ; curls *(hair)*
caramelos *mpl* toffees
caranguejo *m* crab
carapau *m* horse-mackerel
caravana *f* caravan

156

carburador *m* carburettor
carga *f* refill ; load
caril *m* curry
carioca *m* weak coffee
  carioca de limão lemon infusion
carne *f* meat
  carne de borrego spring lamb
  carne picada mince
  carne de porco pork
  carne de vaca beef
  carne de vitela veal
  carnes frias cold meats
carneiro *m* mutton ; lamb
caro(a) dear ; expensive
carrinha *f* van
carrinho *m* trolley
  carrinho de bebé pram ; carry cot
carro *m* car
carruagem *f* carriage *(railway)*
  carruagem-cama sleeper *(railway)*
carruagem-restaurante *f* restaurant car
carta *f* letter
cartão *m* card ; business card
  cartão bancário cheque card
  cartão de crédito credit card
  cartão de embarque boarding card
  cartão de felicitações greetings card
  cartão garantia cheque card
carteira *f* wallet
carteirista *m* pickpocket
carteiro *m* postman
carvão *m* coal
casa *f* home ; house
  casa de banho toilet ; bathroom
casaco *m* jacket ; coat
casado(a) married
casal *m* couple
casamento *m* wedding

caso *m* case
  em caso de... in case of...
castanha *f* chestnut
  castanhas assadas roast chestnuts
  castanhas piladas dried chestnuts
castanho(a) brown
castelo *m* castle
catedral *f* cathedral
causa *f* cause
  por causa de because
cautela take care
cavala *f* mackerel
cavalheiro *m* gentleman

  cavalheiros gents'

cavalo *m* horse
cave (c/v) *f* cellar ; basement
cebola *f* onion
cedo early
cego(a) *m/f* blind *(person)*
ceia *f* supper
célebre famous
cem one hundred
cemitério *m* cemetery
cenoura *f* carrot
centígrado *m* centigrade
centímetro *m* centimetre
cento: por cento per cent
centro *m* centre
  centro da cidade city centre
  centro comercial shopping centre
  centro de saúde health centre
cera *f* wax
cerâmica *f* pottery
cérebro *m* brain
cereja *f* cherry
certeza *f* certainty
  ter a certeza to be sure

certificado m certificate
certo(a) right (correct, accurate) ; certain
cerveja f beer ; lager
  cerveja preta bitter (beer)
cervejaria f beer house
cesto m basket
céu m sky
chá f tea
  chá de limão lemon tea
chamada f telephone call
  chamada gratuita free call
  chamada internacional international call
  chamada pagável no destino reverse charge call
chamar to call
champô m shampoo
chão m floor
chapa de matrícula f number plate
chapéu m hat
  chapéu de sol sunhat
charcutaria f delicatessen
chave f key
  fechar à chave to lock up
chávena f cup
chefe m boss
  chefe de cozinha chef
chega! that's enough!

CHEGADAS ARRIVALS

chegar to arrive
cheio(a) full
cheirar to smell
cheiro m smell
  mau cheiro bad smell
cheque m cheque
  cheque de viagem traveller's cheque
  levantar um cheque to cash a cheque

cherne m black jewfish or grouper
chispalhada f bean stew with pig's trotters
chispe m pig's trotters
chocos mpl cuttlefish
  chocos com tinta cuttlefish cooked in their ink
chouriço m spicy sausage
churrascaria f barbecue restaurant
churrasco m barbecue
  no churrasco barbecued
chuva f rain
chuveiro m shower (bath)
Cia. see companhia
cidadão (cidadã) m/f citizen
cidade f town ; city
cigarro m cigarette
cima : em cima de on (top of)
cinco five
cinto m belt
  cinto de salvação lifebelt
  cinto de segurança seat belt
cinzento(a) grey
circuito m circuit
circular f roundabout (for traffic)
cirurgia f surgery (operation)
claro(a) light (colour) ; bright
classe f class
cliente m/f client
clínica f clinic
clube m club
cobertor m blanket
cobrar to cash
cobrir to cover
código m code ; dialling code
  código postal postcode
codorniz f quail
coelho m rabbit
coentro m coriander
cofre m safe

cogumelo *m* mushroom

coisa *f* thing

cola *f* glue

colar *n* necklace

colar *vb* to stick

colcha *f* bedspread

colchão *m* mattress

colecção *f* collection *(of stamps etc)*

colégio *m* school

colete de salvação *m* life jacket

colher *f* spoon

colina *f* hill

collants *mpl* tights

colorau *m* paprika

coluna *f* pillar
  coluna vertebral spine

com with

comandos *mpl* controls

comboio *m* train

combustível *m* fuel

começar to begin ; to start

comer to eat

comida *f* food

comissário de bordo *m* steward ; purser

como as ; how
  como disse? I beg your pardon?
  como está? how are you?

comodidade *f* comfort

companhia (Cia.) *f* company

compartimento *m* compartment

completar to complete

completo no vacancies

compota *f* jam

compra *f* purchase
  ir às compras to go shopping

comprar to buy

compreender to understand

comprido(a) long

comprimento *m* length

comprimido *m* pill ; tablet

computador *m* computer

concelho *m* council

concordar to agree

concorrente *m/f* candidate

concurso *m* competition

condução *f* driving
  a carta de condução driving licence

condutor *m* driver ; chauffeur

conduzir to drive

conferência *f* conference

conferir to check

congelado(a) frozen *(food)*

congelar to freeze
  não congelar do not freeze

conhaque *m* cognac

conhecer to know *(person, place)*

conselho *m* advice

consertos *mpl* repairs

conservar to keep ; to preserve
  conservar no frio store in a cold place

constipação *f* cold *(illness)*

consulado *m* consulate

consulta *f* consultation ; appointment

consultório *m* surgery

consumir antes de ... best before ... *(label on food)*

conta *f* account; bill

contador *m* meter *(electricity, water)*

conter to contain
  não contem... does not contain...

conto *m* = 1000 escudos

contra against

contraceptivo *m* contraceptive

contrato *m* contract

convidado(a) *m/f* guest

convidar to invite ; to ask *(invite)*

convite m invitation
copo m glass (container)
cor f colour
coração m heart
cordeiro m lamb
cor-de-laranja orange (colour)
cor-de-rosa pink
corpo m body
correia f strap
  correia de ventoinha fan belt
correio m post office
  pelo correio by post
corrente f chain ; current
correr to flow ; to run (person)
correspondência f mail
corrida f bullfight
  corridas de cavalos races
cortar to cut ; to cut off
  cortar e fazer brushing cut and blow-dry
corte m cut
cortiça f cork
costa f shore ; coastline
costela f rib
costeleta f chop (meat) ; cutlet
cotovelo m elbow
couro m leather
couve f cabbage
  couves-de-Bruxelas Brussels sprouts
couve-flor f cauliflower
coxia f aisle
cozer to boil
cozido(a) boiled
  mal cozido underdone
cozinha f kitchen
cozinhar to cook
cozinheiro(a) m/f cook
cravinhos mpl cloves
cravo m carnation
creme m custard

creme de barbear shaving cream
creme para bronzear suntan cream
creme hidratante moisturizer
creme de limpeza cleansing cream
criança f child
cru(a) raw
cruz f cross
cruzamento m junction (crossroads)
cruzar to cross
cruzeiro m cruise
cuecas fpl briefs ; pants
cuidado m care (caution)
cumprimento m greeting
  cumprimentos regards
curso m course
curto(a) short
curva f bend ; turning ; curve
  curva perigosa dangerous bend
custar to cost
custo m charge ; cost
c/v see cave

D

damasco m apricot
dança f dance
dano m damage
Dão fruity red and white wines from the north of Portugal
dar to give
  dar prioridade to give way
data f date
  data de nascimento date of birth
de of ; from
debaixo de under
decidir to decide
dedo m finger

dedo do pé toe
defeito m flaw
deficiente disabled ; handicapped
degrau m step (stair)
deitar-se to lie down
deixar to let (allow) ; to leave behind
delito m crime
demais too much ; too many
demasia f change (money) ; excess
demorado(a) late
demorar to delay
dente m tooth
dentes teeth
dentes postiços false teeth
dentista m dentist
dentro inside
depois after(wards)
depósito m deposit (in bank)
  depósito de bagagens left-luggage
  o depósito da gasolina petrol tank
depressa quickly
desafio m match ; game (sport) ; challenge
desaparecido(a) missing
desapertar to loosen
descafeinado m decaffeinated
descansar to rest
descartável throw-away ; disposable
descer to go down
descoberta f discovery
descongelar to defrost (food) ; to de-ice
desconhecido(a) m/f stranger
desconhecido(a) adj unknown
desconto m discount ; reduction
desculpe excuse me ; sorry
desejar to desire ; to wish

desembarcar to disembark
desempregado(a) unemployed
desenho m design ; drawing
desinchar to go down (swelling)
desinfectante m disinfectant
desligado(a) off (engine, gas)
desligar to hang up (phone) ; to switch off (engine, radio)
desligue o motor switch off your engine
desmaiar to faint
desodorizante m deodorant
despachante m shipper ; transport agent
despesa f expense
desporto m sport
destinatário m addressee
desvio m bypass ; detour ; diversion
detergente m detergent
detergente para a louça washing-up liquid
detergente para a roupa washing powder
devagar slowly ; slow down (sign)
dever: eu devo I must
deve-me... you owe me...
devolver to give back ; to return

DEZEMBRO DECEMBER

dia m day
  dias da semana weekdays
  dia útil working day
  dia de anos birthday
diabético(a) diabetic
diante de in front of (place)
diário daily
diarreia f diarrhoea
dieta f diet ; special regime
diferença f difference
difícil difficult

d

digestão f digestion
diluir to dilute
diminuir to reduce
dínamo m dynamo
dinheiro m money ; cash
direcção f direction ; address ; steering
directo(a) direct
direita f right(-hand side)
 à direita on the right
 para a direita to the right
direito(a) straight ; right(-hand)
 Dto. on right-hand side (address)
direitos mpl duty (tax) ; rights
dirigir to direct
disco m record (music, etc)
 disco de estacionamento parking disk
disponível available
dissolver to dissolve
distância f distance
distrito m district
divã-cama m bed-settee
diversões fpl entertainment
divertir-se to enjoy oneself ; to have fun
dívida f debt
divisas fpl foreign currency
dizer to say
dobrada f tripe
dobrado(a) bent
dobro m double
doce adj sweet (taste)
doce m dessert ; jam
documentos mpl documents
doente ill ; sick
doer to ache ; to hurt
dólar m dollar
domicílio m residence

DOMINGO SUNDAY

dono(a) m/f owner
 dona de casa housewife
dor f ache ; pain
dormir to sleep
Douro region producing port
Dto. see direito(a)
duche m shower
duplo(a) double
durante during
durar to last
duro(a) hard ; stiff ; tough (meat)
dúzia f dozen

E

e and
é he/she/it is ; you are
economizar to save
écrã m screen
edifício m building
edredão m duvet ; quilt
educado(a) polite
eixo de roda m axle
ela she ; her ; it
elástico m elastic band
ele he ; him ; it
eles they (masculine)
electricista m electrician
eléctrico m tram
electrodomésticos mpl electrical appliances
elevador m lift
em at ; in (with towns, countries) ; into
embaixada f embassy
embarcar to board (ship, plane)
embarque m embarkation ; time of sailing
embraiagem f clutch

162

ementa *f* menu

emergência *f* emergency

empregado(a) *m/f* waiter(ess) ; maid ; attendant *(at petrol station)* ; assistant *(in shop)* ; office worker

emprego *m* job ; employment

empurrar to push

EMPURRE PUSH

EN *see* estrada

encaracolado(a) curly

encarnado(a) red

encerrado(a) closed

encher to fill up ; to pump up *(tyre)*

enchidos *mpl* processed meats ; sausages

encomenda *f* parcel

encontrar to meet ; to find

encontro *m* date ; meeting

encosta *f* hill *(slope)*

endereço *m* address

energia *f* energy

o corte de energia power cut

enfermeiro(a) *m/f* nurse

enganar-se to make a mistake

engano *m* mistake

engolir to swallow

NÃO ENGOLIR DO NOT SWALLOW

engraxar to polish *(shoes)*

enguia *f* eel

enjoar to be sick

ensinar to teach

ensopado *m* stew served on slice of bread

enorme big ; huge

entender to understand

entorse *f* sprain

entrada *f* entrance ; starter *(in meal)*

ENTRADA LIVRE ADMISSION FREE

entrar to go in ; to come in ; to get into *(car, etc)*

entre among ; between

entregar to deliver

entrevista *f* interview

enviar to send

enxaqueca *f* migraine

época *f* period

equipamento *m* equipment

equitação *f* horse riding

erro *m* mistake

erva *f* grass ; herb

ervilhas *fpl* peas

esc. *see* escudo

escada *f* ladder ; stairs

escada rolante escalator

escalfado(a) poached *(egg)*

escape *m* exhaust

escocês (escocesa) Scottish

Escócia *f* Scotland

escola *f* school

escova *f* brush

escova de dentes toothbrush

escrever to write

escrito: por escrito in writing

escritório *m* office

escudo (esc.) *m* escudo *(Portuguese currency)*

escuro(a) dark *(colour)*

escutar to listen to

esferográfica *f* ballpoint pen

esgotado(a) sold out *(tickets)* ; exhausted

esgoto *m* drain

esmalte *m* enamel

espaço *m* space

espadarte *m* swordfish

espalhar to scatter

Espanha *f* Spain

espanhol(a) Spanish

espargo m asparagus

esparguete m spaghetti

esparregado m puréed spinach

especialidade f speciality

especiarias fpl spices

espectáculo m show (in theatre etc)

espelho m mirror
  espelho retrovisor driving mirror

esperar to expect ; to hope
  esperar por to wait for

espetada f kebab

espinafre m spinach

esplanada f terrace

esposa f wife

espumante m sparkling wine

espumoso(a) sparkling (wine)

Esq. see esquerda

esquadra f police station

esquentador m water heater

esquerda f left(-hand side)
  à esquerda on the left
  Esq. on left(-hand) side (address)

esqui m ski

esquina f corner (outside)

está he/she/it is ; you are

estação f station
  estação alta high season
  estação do ano season
  estação baixa low season
  estação do comboio railway station
  estação de serviço service station

estacionamento m parking

estacionar to park (car)

estádio m stadium

estado m state
  estado civil marital status

Estados Unidos (EUA) mpl United States

estalagem f inn

estância termal f spa

estar to be

este/esta m/f this
  estes/estas m/f these

estômago m stomach
  o mal-estar de estômago stomach upset

estores mpl blinds

estrada f road
  estrada em mau estado uneven road surface
  estrada nacional (EN) major road ; national highway
  estrada sem saída no through road
  estrada secundária minor road

estrangeiro(a) m/f foreigner

estranho(a) strange

estreito(a) narrow

estudante m/f student

estufado(a) braised

etiqueta f ticket ; label ; etiquette

eu I

EUA see Estados Unidos

europeu (europeia) European

evitar to avoid

excepto except
  excepto aos domingos Sundays excepted

excesso de bagagem m excess luggage

excursão f excursion ; tour
  excursão guiada guided tour

exemplo m example
  por exemplo for example

expirar to expire

explicar to explain

exportação f exportation

exportar to export

exposição f exhibition

extintor m fire extinguisher

extremidade f edge ; extremity

F

fábrica f factory
fabricado(a) em ... made in ...
faca f knife
fácil easy
facilidade f facility ; ease
factura f invoice
fado m traditional Portuguese song
faiança f pottery
faisão m pheasant
faixa f lane (in road)
falar to speak
falecido(a) deceased
falésias fpl cliffs
falta f lack
  falta de corrente power cut
família f family
farinha f flour
farinheira f sausage made with
  pork fat and flour
farmácia f chemist's
  farmácia permanente duty
  chemist
  farmácias de serviço emergency
  chemists'
faróis mpl headlights
farol m headlight ; lighthouse
farolim m sidelight
fatia f slice
fato m suit (man's)
  fato de banho swimsuit
  fato de treino track suit
favas fpl broad beans
favor m favour
  por favor please
  faz favor please
fazer to do ; to make
febras de porco fpl thin slices of
  roast pork
febre f fever

febre dos fenos hay fever

FECHADO CLOSED

  fechado para férias closed for
  holidays
fechar to shut ; to close
feijão m beans
feijão-verde m French beans
feijoada f bean stew with pork
  and spicy sausage
feio(a) awful ; ugly
feira f fair (commercial) ; market
feito(a) à mão handmade
feliz happy
feriado m public holiday
  feriado nacional bank holiday

FERIADOS HOLIDAY/SUNDAYS

férias fpl holidays
ferido(a) injured
ferragens fpl ironware
ferro m iron
  ferro de engomar iron (for clothes)
ferver to boil
festa f party (celebration)

FEVEREIRO FEBRUARY

fiambre m ham
ficar to stay ; to be ; to remain
  ficar bem to suit
ficha f plug (electrical) ; registration
  card (in hotel, clinic)
  ficha dupla/tripla adaptor (electrical)
fígado m liver
figo m fig
  figos secos dried figs
fila f row (line) ; queue
filete m fillet steak ; tenderloin
filha f daughter
filho m son

f filial *f* branch *(of bank, etc)*
filigranas *fpl* filigree work
fim *m* end
  fim-de-semana weekend
fio *m* wire
fita *f* tape ; ribbon
  fita métrica tape measure
flor *f* flower
floresta *f* forest
florista *f* florist
fogão *m* cooker
fogo *m* fire
  fogo de artifício fireworks
folha *f* leaf
  folha de alumínio silver foil
  folha de estanho tinfoil
folhados *mpl* puff pastries
folheto *m* leaflet
fome *f* hunger
  tenho fome I'm hungry
fonte *f* fountain ; source
fora out ; outside
força *f* power *(strength)* ; force
formiga *f* ant
fornecer to supply
forno *m* oven
fortaleza *f* fortress
forte strong
forte *f* fortress
fósforo *m* match
fotografia *f* photograph ; print
fraco(a) weak
fralda *f* nappy
framboesa *f* raspberry
França *f* France
francês (francesa) French
frango *m* chicken *(young and tender)*
frase *f* sentence
freguês (freguesa) *m/f* customer
frente *f* front

em frente de in front of ; opposite
fresco(a) fresh ; cool ; crisp
frigorífico *m* fridge

| FRIO COLD |

fritar to fry
frito(a) fried
fronha *f* pillow case
fronteira *f* border *(frontier)*
fruta *f* fruit
frutaria *f* fruit shop
fruto *m* fruit
fuga *f* leak

| fumadores smokers |

  para não fumadores non-smoking *(compartment, etc)*
fumar to smoke
  não fumar no smoking
fumo *m* smoke
funcionar to work *(machine)*

| não funciona out of order |

funcionário(a) *m/f* employee ; civil servant
fundo *m* bottom
fundo(a) deep
furar to pierce
furnas *fpl* caverns
furto *m* theft
fusível *m* fuse
futebol *m* football

G

gabinete de provas *m* changing room
gado *m* cattle
  gado bravo beware – unfenced bulls

gaivota *f* seagull ; pedal boat
galão *m* large white coffee ; gallon
galeria *f* gallery
Gales : o País de Gales Wales
galês (galesa) Welsh
galinha *f* hen ; chicken
gamba *f* prawn
ganhar to earn ; to win
ganso *m* goose
garagem *f* garage
garantia *f* guarantee

GARE PLATFORM

garfo *m* fork
garganta *f* throat
garoto *m* boy ; small white coffee
garrafa *f* bottle
garrafão *m* two or five-litre bottle
gás *m* gas
  a botija de gás gas cylinder
gasóleo *m* diesel
gasolina *f* petrol
gasosa *f* fizzy sweetened water
gastar to spend
gaveta *f* drawer
gelado *m* ice cream ; ice lolly
gelar to freeze
gelataria *f* ice cream parlour
geleia *f* jelly
gelo *m* ice
gémeo(a) twin
género *m* kind ; type
gengibre *m* ginger
gengivas *fpl* gums
gente *f* people
  toda a gente everybody
geral *f* gallery *(in theatre)*
geral *adj* general
  em geral generally
geralmente usually

gerente *m* manager
ginjinha *f* morello cherry liqueur
gira-discos *m* record player
girassol *m* sunflower
gola *f* collar
golfe *m* golf
  o taco de golfe golf club *(stick)*
gordo(a) fat
gorjeta *f* tip *(to waiter, etc)*
gostar de to like
gosto *m* taste
governo *m* government
Grã-Bretanha *f* Britain
grama *m* gramme
grande big ; large ; great
grão *m* chickpeas
grátis free *(costing nothing)*
gravador *m* tape recorder
gravata *f* tie
grávida pregnant
gravura *f* print *(picture)*
grelhado(a) grilled
greve *f* strike *(industrial)*
  em greve on strike
gripe *f* flu
groselha *f* (red)currant
grosso(a) thick
grupo *m* group ; party *(group)*
  grupo sanguíneo blood group
grutas *fpl* caves
guarda *m/f* police officer
guarda-chuva *m* umbrella
guarda-lamas *m* mudguard
guardanapo *m* napkin
guardar to keep ; to watch over
guarda-sol *m* sunshade
guia *m/f* guide
guiché *m* window *(at post office, bank)*
guisado *m* stew
guitarra *f* guitar

g

g

g

H

há there is ; there are
habitação f residence ; home
habitar to reside
história f history ; story
hoje today
homem m man

hora f hour ; time *(by the clock)*
  hora de chegada time of arrival
  hora de partida departure time
  hora de ponta rush hour

hortelã f mint *(herb)*
hortelã-pimenta f peppermint
hóspede m/f guest
hospedeira f hostess
  hospedeira de bordo flight
  attendant

I

iate m yacht
icterícia f jaundice
ida f visit ; trip
  ida e volta return trip
idade f age
identificação f identification
idosos mpl the elderly ; old people
ignição f ignition ; starter *(in car)*
igreja f church
igual equal ; the same as
ilha f island
impedir to prevent
impedido(a) engaged *(phone)*
imperial m draught beer
impermeável m raincoat ; water-

proof
importação f importation
importância f importance ;
  amount *(money)*
importante important
imposto m tax ; duty
  impostos duty ; tax
impressão digital f fingerprint
impresso m form *(to fill in)*
imprevisto(a) unexpected
impulso m unit of charge *(for phone)*
incêndio m fire
inchado(a) swollen
incluído(a) included
incomodar to disturb
  não incomodar do not disturb
indicativo m dialling code
indigestão f indigestion
infecção f infection
infeccioso(a) infectious *(illness)*
inflamação f inflammation

infracção f offence
Inglaterra f England
inglês (inglesa) English
iniciais fpl initials
iniciar to begin
início m beginning
inquilino m tenant
inscrever to register
insecto m insect
insolação f heatstroke ; sunstroke
instalações fpl facilities
instituto m institute
insuflável inflatable
inteiro(a) whole
interdito(a) forbidden
interessante interesting
interior inside

interno(a) internal
intérprete *m/f* interpreter
interruptor *m* switch
intervalo *m* interval *(in theatre)*
intestinos *mpl* bowels
intoxicação *f* food poisoning
introduzir to introduce
inundação *f* flood
inverno *m* winter
iogurte *m* yoghurt
ir to go
Irlanda *f* Ireland
  a Irlanda do Norte Northern Ireland
irlandês (irlandesa) Irish
irmã *f* sister
irmão *m* brother
iscas *fpl* marinated pig's liver with potatoes
isqueiro *m* lighter
isso that
isto this
Itália *f* Italy
italiano(a) Italian
itinerário *m* route ; itinerary
IVA *m* VAT

J

já already ; now

JANEIRO JANUARY

janela *f* window
jantar *m* dinner ; evening meal
jardim *m* garden
joalharia *f* jeweller's ; jewellery
joelho *m* knee
jogar to play
jogo *m* match ; game; play
jóia *f* jewel

jornal *m* newspaper
jovem young

JULHO JULY

JUNHO JUNE

juntar to join
junto near
juventude *f* youth

K

kg. *see* quilo(grama)

L

lã *f* wool
lábio *m* lip
laço *m* bow *(ribbon, string)*
lado *m* side
  ao lado de next to
ladrão *m* thief
lagarto *m* lizard
lago *m* lake
lagosta *f* lobster
lagostim *m* king prawn
lâminas de barbear *fpl* razor blades
lâmpada *f* light bulb
lampreia *f* lamprey eel
lançar to throw
lanchar to go for snack/light lunch
lanche *m* light afternoon meal ; snack
lápis *m* pencil
  lápis de cera crayons *(wax)*
lar *m* home
laranja *f* orange
  o doce de laranja marmalade
largo *m* small square

largo(a) broad ; loose *(clothes)* ; wide
largura *f* width
lata *f* tin ; can *(of food)*
latão *m* brass
lavabo *m* lavatory ; toilet
lava-louça *m* sink
lavandaria *f* laundry
  lavandaria automática launderette
  lavandaria a seco dry-cleaner's
lavar to wash *(clothes, etc)*
lavar a louça to wash up
lavar à mão to handwash
lavável washable
lebre *f* hare
legumes *mpl* vegetables
lei *f* law
leilão *m* auction
leitão *m* sucking pig
leite *m* milk
  com leite white *(coffee)*
  leite desnatado skimmed milk
  leite evaporado evaporated milk
  leite gordo full cream milk
  leite de limpeza cleansing milk
  leite magro skimmed milk
  leite meio gordo semi-skimmed milk
lembranças *fpl* souvenirs
lembrar-se to remember
leme *m* rudder ; helm
lenço *m* handkerchief ; tissue
lençol *m* sheet
lente *f* lens
  lentes de contacto contact lenses
lento(a) slow
leque *m* fan *(hand-held)*
ler to read
leste *m* east

letra *f* letter *(of alphabet)*
  letra maiúscula capital letter
levantar to draw *(money)* ; to lift
levantar-se to stand up ; get up *(from bed)*
levar to take ; to carry
leve light *(not heavy)*
libra *f* pound
  libras esterlinas pounds sterling
lição *f* lesson
licença *f* permit
liceu *m* secondary school
licor *m* liqueur
ligação *f* connection *(trains, etc)*
ligado(a) on *(engine, gas, etc)*
ligeiro(a) light
lima *f* lime *(fruit)*
lima *f* file
  lima das unhas nailfile
limão *m* lemon
limite *m* limit
  limite de velocidade speed limit
limonada *f* lemonade
limpar to wipe ; to clean
limpeza *f* cleaning
  limpeza a seco dry-cleaning
limpo(a) clean
língua *f* language ; tongue
linguado *m* sole *(fish)*
linguiça *f* narrow spicy pork sausage
linha *f* line ; thread ; platform *(railway)*
linho *m* linen
liquidação *f* (clearance) sale
Lisboa (Lx) Lisbon
liso(a) smooth ; straight
lista *f* list
  lista de preços price list
  lista telefónica telephone directory

litro m litre
livraria f bookshop

LIVRE FREE/VACANT/FOR HIRE

livro m book
lixívia f bleach
lixo m rubbish
loção f lotion
loja f shop
lombo m loin (cut of meat)
Londres London
longe far
  é longe? is it far?
longo(a) long
lotaria f lottery
louça f dishes ; crockery
louro(a) fair (hair)
louro m bay leaf (herb)
lua f moon
lua-de-mel f honeymoon
lugar m seat (theatre) ; place
lulas fpl squid
luvas fpl gloves
luxo m luxury
luz f light
  luzes de presença sidelights
  luzes de perigo hazard lights
Lx see Lisboa

M

M. underground (metro)
má see mau
maçã f apple
maçaroca f corn on the cob
macho m male (animal)
macio(a) soft ; smooth
maço m packet (of cigarettes)
madeira f wood
Madeira f island renowned for its

fortified wines
madrugada f early morning
maduro(a) ripe
mãe f mother
magro(a) thin

MAIO MAY

maior larger
  a maior parte de the majority of
mais more
  o/a mais the most
mal wrong ; evil
mala f suitcase ; bag ; trunk
malagueta f chilli
mal-entendido m misunderstanding
mal-estar m discomfort
mancha f stain
mandar to send ; to order
maneira f way (method)
manga f sleeve ; mango
manhã f morning
manteiga f butter
manter to keep ; to maintain
mão f hand
mapa m map
  mapa das estradas road map
  mapa das ruas street plan
máquina f machine
  máquina fotográfica camera
mar m sea
maracujá m passion fruit
marca f brand ; mark
marcação f booking ; dialling
marcar to dial (phone) ; to mark
marcha-atrás f reverse (gear)

MARÇO MARCH

marco do correio m pillar box
maré f tide
maré-baixa f low tide

m

m

m

maré-cheia f high tide
marfim m ivory
marido m husband
marisco m seafood ; shellfish
marmelada f quince jelly
marmelo m quince
mármore m marble (substance)
Marrocos Morocco
marroquinaria f leather goods
mas but
massa f dough
  massas pasta
  massa folhada puff pastry
matrícula f number plate
mau (má) bad ; evil
máximo(a) maximum
mazagrã m iced coffee and lemon
me me
mecânico m mechanic
média f average
medicamento m medicine
médico(a) m/f doctor
medida f measure ; size
médio(a) medium
medusa f jellyfish
meia f stocking ; half
meia-hora f half-hour
meia-noite f midnight
meio m middle
  no meio de in the middle of
meio(a) half
  meia garrafa a half bottle
  meia de leite cup of milky coffee
  meia pensão half board
meio-dia m midday ; noon
meio-seco medium sweet (wine)
mel m honey
melancia f watermelon
melão m melon
melhor best ; better

meloa f small round melon
menina f Miss ; girl
menino m boy
menor smaller ; minor (underage)
menos least ; less
mensagem f message
mensal monthly
menstruação f period (menstruation)
mercado m market
mercearia f grocer's
merengue m meringue
mês m month
mesa f table
mesmo(a) same
mesquita f mosque
metade f half
  metade do preço half price
meter to put in
metro m metre ; underground (rail)
metropolitano m tube (underground)
meu (minha) my ; mine
mexer to move

NÃO MEXER DO NOT TOUCH

mexilhão m mussel
migas à alentejana thick bread
  soup
mil thousand
milhão m million
milho m maize ; corn
mim me
minha see meu
mínimo(a) minimum
minúsculo(a) tiny
mobília f furniture
mochila f backpack ; rucksack
moda f fashion
moeda f coin ; currency
moído(a) ground (coffee, etc)
moinho m windmill

moinho de café coffee grinder

mola *f* peg ; spring *(coiled metal)*

molhado(a) wet

molho *m* sauce ; gravy

momento *m* moment

montanha *f* mountain

montante *m* amount *(total)*

montra *f* shop window

morada *f* address

moradia *f* villa

morango *m* strawberry

morar to live ; to reside

morcela *f* black pudding

mordedura de insecto *f* insect bite

morder to bite

moreno(a) tanned ; dark skinned

morrer to die

mortadela *f* cold meat

mosaicos *mpl* mosaic tiles

mosca *f* fly *(insect)*

mostarda *f* mustard

mosteiro *m* monastery

mostrador *m* dial ; glass counter

mostrar to show

motocicleta *f* motorbike

motor *m* engine ; motor
  motor de arranque starter motor

motorista *m* driver

motorizada *f* motorbike

muçulmano(a) Muslim

mudar to change
  mudar-se to move house

muito very ; much ; quite *(rather)*

muitos(as) a lot (of) ; many ; plenty (of)

mulher *f* female ; woman ; wife

multa *f* fine

multidão *f* crowd

mundial worldwide

mundo *m* world

muralhas *fpl* ramparts

muro *m* wall

museu *m* museum

música *f* music

N

nabo *m* turnip

nacional national

nacionalidade *f* nationality ; citizenship

nada nothing
  nada a declarar nothing to declare

nadar to swim

namorada *f* girlfriend

namorado *m* boyfriend

não no ; not

nariz *m* nose

nascer to be born

nascimento *m* birth

nata *f* cream

natação *f* swimming

Natal *m* Christmas

naturalidade *f* place of birth

natureza *f* nature

navio *m* ship

neblina *f* mist

negar to refuse

negativo(a) negative

negócios *mpl* business

negro(a) black

nem: nem... nem... neither... nor...

nenhum(a) none

neta *f* granddaughter

neto *m* grandson

n

neve f snow
nevoeiro m fog
ninguém nobody
nível m level
nó m knot
  nó rodoviário motorway junction
No. see número
nocivo(a) harmful
nódoa f stain
noite f evening ; night
  à noite in the evening
  boa noite good evening/night
noivo(a) engaged to be married
nome m name
  nome próprio first name
nora f daughter-in-law
nordeste m north east
normalmente usually
noroeste m north west
norte m north
nós we ; us
nosso(a) our
nota f note ; banknote
notar to notice
notícia f piece of news
Nova Zelândia f New Zealand

novo(a) new ; young ; recent
noz f nut ; walnut
noz-moscada f nutmeg
nu(a) naked
nublado(a) dull (weather) ; cloudy
número (No.) m number ; size (of clothes, shoes)
nunca never
nuvem f cloud

O

o the (masculine)
objecto m object
  objectos perdidos lost property
obra-prima f masterpiece
obras fpl roadworks ; repairs
obrigado(a) thank you
oceano m ocean
ocidental western
oculista m optician
óculos mpl glasses
  óculos de sol sunglasses

oeste m west
oferecer to offer ; to give something
oferta f offer ; gift
olá hello
olaria f pottery
óleo m oil
  óleo dos travões brake fluid
oleoso(a) greasy ; oily
olhar para/por to look at/after
olho m eye
onda f wave (on sea)
onde where
ontem yesterday
óptimo(a) excellent
ora now ; well now
orçamento m budget
ordem f order
ordenado m wage
orelha f ear
organizado(a) organized
orquídea f orchid
osso m bone
ostra f oyster

ou or

ourivesaria e joalharia goldsmith's and jeweller's

ouro *m* gold
  de ouro gold *(made of gold)*

outono *m* autumn

outro(a) other
  outra vez again

ouvido *m* ear

ouvir to hear ; to listen (to)

ovelha *f* sheep

ovo *m* egg

oxigénio *m* oxygen

P

padaria *f* baker's

pagamento *m* payment
  pagamento a pronto cash payment

pagar to pay

página *f* page
  páginas amarelas Yellow Pages

pago(a) paid

pai *m* father
  pais parents

país *m* country

palácio *m* palace

palavra *f* word

pálido(a) pale

palito *m* toothpick

panado(a) fried in egg and breadcrumbs

pane *f* breakdown *(car)*

panela *f* pan ; pot

pano *m* cloth

pão *m* bread ; loaf
  pão de centeio rye bread
  pão integral wholemeal bread

pão de ló sponge cake
  pão de milho maize bread
  pão torrado toasted bread
  pão de trigo wheat bread

papel *m* paper
  papel de carta writing paper
  papel de embrulho wrapping paper
  papel higiénico toilet paper

papelaria *f* stationer's

papo-seco *m* roll *(of bread)*

par *m* pair ; couple

para for ; towards ; to

parabéns *mpl* congratulations ; happy birthday

pára-brisas *f* windscreen

pára-choques *m* bumper

parafuso *m* screw

paragem *f* stop *(for bus, etc)*

parar to stop

pare stop *(sign)*
  pare ao sinal vermelho stop when lights are red

parede *f* wall

parente *m* relation *(family)*

pargo *m* sea bream

parque *m* park

parquímetro *m* parking meter

parte *f* part
  parte de frente front
  parte de trás back

particular private

partir to break ; to leave
  a partir de ... from ...

Páscoa *f* Easter

passa *f* raisin

passadeira *f* zebra crossing

passado *m* the past

passado(a): mal passado rare *(steak)*

bem passado well done *(steak)*
passageiro *m* passenger
passagem *f* fare ; crossing
  passagem de nível level-crossing
  passagem de peões pedestrian crossing
  passagem proibida no right of way
  passagem subterrânea underpass
passaporte *m* passport
passar to pass ; to go by
pássaro *m* bird
passatempos *mpl* hobbies
passe *m* season ticket
passe go *(when crossing road)* ; walk
passear to go for a walk
passeio *m* walk ; pavement
pasta *f* paste
  pasta dentífrica toothpaste
pastéis *mpl* pastries

pastel *m* pie ; pastry *(cake)*
  pastel folhado puff pastry
pastelaria *f* pastries ; café ; cake shop
pastilha *f* pastille
  pastilha elástica chewing gum
  pastilhas para a garganta throat lozenges
pataniscas *fpl* salted cod fritters
patinagem *f* skating *(ice)* ; roller-skating
patinar to skate
pátio *m* courtyard
pato *m* duck
pau *m* stick
pé *m* foot
  a pé on foot

peão *m* pedestrian
peça *f* part ; play
  peças e acessórios spares and accessories

peça... ask for...
pediatra *m/f* paediatrician
pedir to ask
  pedir alguma coisa to ask for something
  pedir emprestado to borrow
peito *m* breast ; chest
peixaria *f* fishmonger's
peixe *m* fish
  peixe congelado frozen fish
peixe-espada *m* scabbard fish
pele *f* fur ; skin
película *f* film *(for camera)*
pensão *m* guesthouse
  pensão completa full board
  pensão residencial boarding house
  meia pensão half board
pensar to think
penso *m* sticking plaster
  penso higiénico sanitary towel
pente *m* comb
peões *mpl* pedestrians
pepino *m* cucumber
  pepino de conserva gherkin
pequeno(a) little ; small
  pequeno-almoço breakfast
pera *f* pear
  pera abacate avocado pear
percebes *mpl* edible barnacles
percurso *m* route
perdão I beg your pardon ; I'm sorry
perder to lose ; to miss *(train, etc)*
perdido(a) lost
  perdidos e achados lost and found ; lost property
perdiz *f* partridge
pergunta *f* question
  fazer uma pergunta to ask a question

perigo de incêndio fire hazard
perigoso(a) dangerous
permitir to allow
perna f leg
pérola f pearl
pertencer to belong
perto de near
perú m turkey
pesado(a) heavy
pêsames mpl condolences
pesar to weigh
pesca f fishing
pescada f hake
pescadinhas fpl whiting
pescar to fish
peso m weight
pêssego m peach
pessoa f person
pessoal adj personal
pessoal n staff ; personnel
petiscos mpl snacks ; titbits
petróleo m oil
peúgas fpl socks
picada f sting
picado(a) chopped ; minced
picante spicy
pilha f pile ; battery (for torch)
pílula f the pill
pimenta f pepper
pimento m pepper (vegetable)
pintar to paint
pintura f painting
pior worse
piripiri m hot chilli dressing
pisca-pisca m indicator (on car)
piscina f swimming pool
piscina aberta outdoor swimming pool

piscina para crianças paddling pool
piso m floor ; level ; surface
piso escorregadio slippery surface
pista f track ; runway
planta f plant ; map
plataforma f platform
plateia f stalls (in theatre)
platinados fpl points (in car)
pneu m tyre
a pressão dos pneus tyre pressure
pó m dust ; powder
pó de talco talcum powder
poço m well
poder to be able
polegar m thumb

polícia m policeman ; police officer
mulher-polícia f policewoman
poluição f pollution
polvo m octopus
pomada f ointment
pomada para o calçado shoe polish
pomar m orchard
pombo m pigeon
ponte f bridge
população f population
por by (through)
por aqui/por ali this/that way
por hora per hour
por pessoa per person
pôr to put
porção f portion
porco m pig ; pork
por favor please
pormenores mpl details
porque because

p

porquê why
porta *f* door
  a porta No. ... gate number ...
porta-bagagens *m* boot *(of car)* ;
  luggage rack
porta-chaves *m* key ring

PORTAGEM MOTORWAY TOLL

porta-moedas *m* purse
porteiro *m* porter
porto *m* harbour
Porto : o Porto Oporto
  o vinho do Porto Port wine
português (portuguesa)
  Portuguese
posologia *f* dose *(medicine)*
postal *m* postcard
posto *m* post ; job
  posto clínico first aid post
  posto de socorros first aid centre
pouco(a) little
pousada *f* state-run hotel ; inn
povo *m* people
povoação *f* small village
praça *f* square *(in town)* ; market
  praça de táxis taxi rank
  praça de touros bullring
praia *f* beach ; seaside
prata *f* silver
prateleira *f* shelf
praticar to practise
prato *m* dish ; plate ; course of
  meal
  prato da casa speciality of the
  house
  prato do dia today's special
prazer *m* pleasure
  prazer em conhecê-lo pleased
  to meet you
precipício *m* cliff ; precipice
precisar to need
  é preciso it is necessary

preço *m* price
  preços de ocasião bargain
  prices
  preços reduzidos reduced prices
preencher to fill in
preferir to prefer
prejuízo *m* damage
prémio *m* prize
prenda *f* gift
preocupado(a) worried
preparado(a) ready
presente *m* gift ; present
pressão *f* pressure
  pressão dos pneus tyre pressure
presunto *m* cured ham
preto(a) black
primavera *f* spring *(season)*
primeiro(a) first
  primeiro andar first floor
  de primeira classe first class
primo(a) *m/f* cousin
princípio *m* beginning
prioridade *f* priority
  prioridade à direita give way to
  the right
prisão *f* prison
  ter prisão de ventre to be
  constipated

PRIVADO PRIVATE

procurar to look for
produto *m* product ; proceeds
  produtos alimentares foodstuffs
professor(a) *m/f* teacher
profissão *f* profession
  profissão, idade, nome profession, age and name
profundidade *f* depth
profundo(a) deep

PROIBIDO FORBIDDEN

proibida a entrada no entry
proibido estacionar no parking
proibido fumar no smoking
proibida a paragem no stopping
proibida a passagem no access
proibido pisar a relva do not walk on the grass
proibido tomar banho no bathing
promoção f special offer
pronto(a) ready
propriedade f estate (property)
proprietário(a) m/f owner
prospecto m pamphlet
prótese dentária f dental fittings
provar to taste ; to try on
provisório(a) temporary
próximo(a) near ; next
público m audience ; public
pudim m pudding
pulmão m lung
pulseira f bracelet ; wrist strap
pulso m wrist
pura lã f pure wool
purificador do ar m air freshener
puxar to pull

PUXE PULL

Q

quadro m picture ; painting
qual which
qualidade f quality
quando when
quantidade f quantity
quanto how much
  quantos(as)? how many?
  quanto tempo? how long? (time)

QUARTA-FEIRA WEDNESDAY

quarto m room ; bedroom
  quarto de banho bathroom
  quarto com duas camas twin-bedded room
  quarto de casal double room
  quarto individual single room
quarto fourth ; quarter
  um quarto de hora a quarter of an hour
que what
  o que é? what is it?
quebra-mar m pier
quebrar to break
queda f fall
queijada f cheesecake
queijo m cheese
queimadura f burn
  queimadura do sol sunburn (painful)
queixa f complaint
quem who

QUENTE HOT

querer to want ; to wish
quilo(grama) (kg.) m kilo
quilómetro m kilometre
quinta f farm

QUINTA-FEIRA THURSDAY

quiosque m kiosk ; newsstand
quotidiano(a) daily

R

R. see rua
rã f frog
rabanete m radish
rádio m radio
radiografia f X-ray
raia f skate (fish)
raiva f rabies

179

raíz f root
rapariga f girl
rapaz m boy
rápido m express (train)
rápido(a) fast
raposa f fox
raqueta f racket
rasgar to tear
ratazana f rat
rato m mouse
R/C see rés-do-chão
real real ; royal
reboques mpl breakdown service
rebuçado m sweet (confectionery)
recado m message
  dar um recado to give a message
receber to receive
receita f recipe
  receita médica prescription
recepção f reception
recibo m receipt
reclamação f protest ; complaint
  fazer uma reclamação to make a complaint
recolher to collect
  recolha de bagagem baggage reclaim
recomendar to recommend
recompensa f reward
reconhecer to recognize
recordação f souvenir
recordar-se to remember
rede f net
redução f reduction ; discount
reembolsar to reimburse
refeição f meal
  refeição da casa set menu
reformado(a) m/f senior citizen ; retired
região f area (region)
  região demarcada official wine-producing region
registar to register
regulamentos mpl regulations
Reino Unido m United Kingdom
relógio m watch ; clock
relva f grass
  não pisar a relva keep off grass
remédio m medicine ; remedy
remetente m sender
renda f lace ; rent
  rendas de bilros handwoven lacework
reparação f repair
reparar to fix ; to repair
repartição f state department
repetir to repeat

RÉS-DO-CHÃO (R/C) GROUND FLOOR

reservar to reserve
  reserva de lugar seat reservation
reservado(a) reserved
reservar to book ; to reserve
residência f boarding house ; residence
residir to live
respirar to breathe
responder to answer ; to reply
resposta f answer
restaurante m restaurant
retalho m oddment
retrosaria f haberdashery
reunião f meeting
revelar to develop (photos) ; to reveal
revisor m ticket collector
revista f magazine
ribeiro m stream
rins mpl kidneys
rio m river
rissol m rissole

180

rochas *fpl* rocks
roda *f* wheel
rodovia *f* highway
rolha *f* cork
rolo *m* cartridge *(for camera)* ; roll
rosto *m* face
roteiro *m* guidebook
roubar to steal ; to rob
roupa *f* clothes
  roupa interior underwear
roxo(a) purple
rua (R.) *f* street
rubéola *f* German measles
ruído *m* noise
ruptura *f* break

S

S. *see* São

sabão *m* soap
  sabão em flocos soapflakes
  sabão em pó soap powder
saber to know *(fact)*
sabonete *m* toilet soap
sabor *m* flavour ; taste
saca-rolhas *m* corkscrew
saco *m* bag ; handbag
  saco cama sleeping bag
  saco do lixo bin bag
safio *m* sea eel
saia *f* skirt

SAÍDA EXIT/WAY OUT

  saídas departures
sair to go out ; to come out
sal *m* salt
sala *f* room
  sala de chá tea room ; café
  sala de embarque airport lounge

  sala de espera waiting room
  sala de estar living room ; lounge
  sala de jantar dining room
salada *f* salad
salão *m* hall *(for concerts, etc)*
salário *m* wage ; salary

SALDO SALE

salgado(a) salty
salmão *m* salmon
  salmão fumado smoked salmon
salmonete *m* red mullet
salpicão *m* spicy sausage
salsa *f* parsley
salsicha *f* sausage
salsicharia *f* delicatessen
salteado(a) sautéed
salvar to rescue ; to save *(rescue)*
sandálias *fpl* sandals
sandes *f* sandwich
  sandes de fiambre ham sandwich
sanduíche *f* sandwich
sangue *m* blood

SANITÁRIOS TOILETS

Santo(a) (Sto./Sta.) *m/f* saint
santo(a) holy
santola *f* spider crab
São (S.) *m* Saint
sapataria *f* shoe shop
sapateira *f* type of crab
sapateiro *m* shoemaker ; cobbler
sapato *m* shoe
saquinhos de chá *mpl* tea bags
sarampo *m* measles
sardinha *f* sardine
satisfeito(a) happy ; satisfied
saudação *f* greeting
saudável healthy
saúde *f* health

saúde! cheers!
se if ; whether
  se faz favor (SFF) please
sé f cathedral
secador m dryer
secar to dry ; to drain *(tank)*
secção f department
seco(a) dry
secretária f desk
secretário(a) m/f secretary
século m century
seda f silk
sede f thirst
  ter sede to be thirsty
segredo m secret
seguinte following
seguir to follow
  seguir pela direita keep to your right
  seguir pela esquerda keep to your left

SEGUNDA-FEIRA MONDAY

segundo m second *(time)*
segundo(a) second
  segundo andar second floor
  de segunda classe second class
  em segunda mão second-hand
segurança f safety
segurar to hold
seguro m insurance
  seguro contra terceiros third party insurance
  seguro contra todos os riscos comprehensive insurance
seguro de viagem travel insurance
seguro(a) safe ; reliable
seio m breast
selecção f selection
selo m stamp
selvagem wild

sem without
semáforos mpl traffic lights
semana f week
  para a semana next week
  na semana passada last week
  por semana weekly *(rate, etc)*
semanal weekly
sempre always
senhor m sir ; gentleman ; you
  Senhor Mr
senhora f lady ; madam ; you
  Senhora Mrs, Ms

SENHORAS LADIES'

senhorio(a) m/f landlord/lady
sentar-se to sit (down)
sentido m sense ; meaning
  sentido único one-way street
sentir to feel
ser to be
serviço m service ; cover charge
  serviço de quartos room service
  serviço (não) incluído service (not) included
  serviço permanente 24-hour service
sessão f session ; performance

SETEMBRO SEPTEMBER

seu (sua) his ; her ; your

SEXTA-FEIRA FRIDAY

SFF *see* se faz por favor
shampô m shampoo
significar to mean
sim yes
simpático(a) nice ; friendly
sinal m signal ; deposit *(part payment)*
  sinal de impedido engaged tone
  sinal de marcação dialling tone
  sinal de trânsito road sign
sino m bell

sítio *m* place ; spot

situado(a) situated

só only ; alone

sobre over ; on top of
  sobre o mar overlooking the sea

sobrecarga *f* excess load ; surcharge

sobremesa *f* dessert

sobressalente spare
  a roda sobressalente spare wheel

sobretudo *m* overcoat *(man's)*

sócio *m* member ; partner

socorro *m* help ; assistance
  socorro 115 emergency service
  999
  socorros e sinistrados accidents
  and emergencies

sol *m* sun

solteiro(a) single *(not married)*

solúvel soluble

som *m* sound

soma *f* amount *(sum)*

sombra *f* shadow *(in sun)*

sono *m* sleep

sopa *f* soup

sorte *f* luck ; fortune
  boa sorte good luck

sorvete *m* water-ice ; sorbet

sótão *m* attic

soutien *m* bra

sua *see* seu

subida *f* rise ; ascent

subir to go up

sudeste *m* south east

sudoeste *m* south west

suficiente enough

sujo(a) dirty

sul *m* south

sumo *m* juice

suor *m* sweat

supermercado *m* supermarket

supositório *m* suppository

surdo(a) deaf

surf *m* surfing

T

tabacaria *f* tobacconist's ;
  newsagent

tabaco *m* tobacco

tabela *f* list ; table

taberna *f* wine bar

tabuleiro *m* tray

taça *f* cup

tacão *m* heel

talão *m* voucher

talco *m* talc

talheres *mpl* cutlery

talho *m* butcher's

talvez perhaps

tamanho *m* size

também also ; too

tamboril *m* monkfish

tampa *f* lid ; cover ; top ; cap

tampões *mpl* tampons

tanto(a) so much

tão so

tapete *m* carpet ; rug
  tapetes e carpetes rugs and
  carpets

tarde *f* afternoon
  boa tarde good afternoon

tarde late *(in the day)*

tarifa *f* charge ; rate
  tarifas de portagem toll charges

tarte *f* tart
  tarte de amêndoa almond tart

tasca *f* tavern ; wine bar ;
  restaurant

taxa *f* fee

taxa de juro interest rate
taxa normal peak-time rate
taxa reduzida off-peak rate
teatro m theatre
tecido m fabric ; tissue ; cloth
tejadilho m roof rack
telecomandado(a) remote-controlled
teleférico m cable car
telefone m telephone
telefonista f operator
televisão f television
televisor m television set
telhado m roof
temperatura f temperature
tempero m dressing (for salad) ; seasoning
tempestade f storm

tempo m weather ; time (duration)
tempo inteiro full-time
tempo parcial part-time
temporada f season
temporário(a) temporary
tenda f tent
ténis m tennis
tenro(a) tender (meat)
tensão f tension
tensão arterial alta/baixa high/low blood pressure
tentar to try
ter to have
ter febre to have a temperature

TERÇA-FEIRA TUESDAY

terceiro(a) third
terceiro andar third floor
para a terceira idade for the elderly
termas fpl spa
termo m (vacuum) flask

termómetro m thermometer
terra f earth ; ground
terraço m veranda ; balcony
terramoto m earthquake
terreno m ground ; land
tesoura f scissors
tesouro m treasure
testemunha f witness
tímido(a) shy
tingir to dye
tinta f ink ; paint
tinturaria f dry-cleaner's
tio(a) m/f uncle/aunt
tipo m sort ; kind
tira-nódoas m stain remover
tirar to remove ; to take out
tiro m shot
toalha f towel
toalhete de rosto m face cloth ; flannel (for washing)
toalhetes refrescantes mpl baby wipes
tocar to touch ; to ring ; to play
tocar piano to play the piano
todo(a) all ; the whole
toda a gente everyone
todas as coisas everything
em toda a parte everywhere
toldo f sunshade (on beach)
tomada f socket ; power point
tomar to take
tomar banho to bathe ; to take a bath
tomar antes de se deitar take before going to bed
tomar em jejum take on an empty stomach
tomar... vezes ao dia take... times a day
tomate m tomato
tonelada f ton

toranja f grapefruit
torcer to twist ; to turn
torneio m tournament
torneira f tap
tornozelo m ankle
torrada f toast
torre f tower
torto(a) twisted
tosse f cough
tosta f toasted sandwich
  tosta de queijo toasted cheese sandwich
tostões: 25 tostões = 2.5 escudos
totobola m football pools
totoloto m lottery
toucinho m bacon
tourada f bullfight
touro m bull
tóxico(a) poisonous ; toxic
trabalhar to work (person)
trabalho m work
  trabalhos na estrada roadworks
tradução f translation
traduzir to translate
tráfego m traffic
tranquilo(a) calm ; quiet
transferir to transfer
trânsito m traffic
  trânsito condicionado restricted traffic
  trânsito proibido no entry
transpiração f perspiration ; sweat
transportar to transport ; to carry
transtorno m upset ; inconvenience
trás: para trás backwards
  no banco de trás on the back-seat of car
  a parte de trás back
tratamento m treatment
tratar de to treat ; to deal with

travar to brake
travessa f lane (in town) ; serving dish
travessia f crossing (voyage)
travões mpl brakes
trazer to bring ; to carry
triângulo m warning triangle
tribunal m court
trigo m wheat
triste sad
trocar to exchange ; to change
troco m change (money)
  trocos small change
trovoada f thunderstorm
truta f trout
tu you (informal)
tubo m exhaust pipe ; tube ; hose
tudo everything ; all
turista m/f tourist

U

ultimamente lately ; recently
último(a) last ; latest
ultrapassar to overtake ; to pass
um(a) a ; an ; one
unha f nail (on finger, toe)
único(a) single ; unique
unidade f unit (hi-fi, etc) ; unity
unir to join
universidade f university ; college
urgência f urgency
urtiga f nettle
usado(a) used (car, etc)
usar to use ; to wear
uso m use
  uso externo for external use
útil useful
utilização f use

u

utilizar to use
uva *f* grape

vaca *f* cow
vacina *f* vaccination
vagão *m* railway carriage ; coach
vagão-restaurante *m* buffet car
vagar to be vacant

vale *m* valley
valer to be worth

válido(a) valid
  válido até... valid until...
valor *m* value
válvula *f* valve ; tap
vapor *m* steam
varanda *f* veranda ; balcony
variado(a) varied
varicela *f* chickenpox
vários(as) several
vazio(a) empty
vegetal *m* vegetable
  vegetais congelados frozen vegetables
vegetariano(a) vegetarian
veículo *m* vehicle
  veículos pesados heavy goods vehicles
vela *f* sail ; sailing
vela *f* spark plug ; candle
velho(a) old
velocidade *f* gear ; speed
  velocidade limitada speed limit in force
velocímetro *m* speedometer

vencimento *m* wage ; salary
venda *f* sale *(in general)*
  venda proibida not for public sale
  vendas e reparações sales and repairs
vender to sell

veneno *m* poison
vento *m* wind
ventoinha *f* fan *(electric)*
ver to see ; to look at
verão *m* summer
verdade *f* truth
  não é verdade? isn't it?
verdadeiro(a) true
verde green
vergas *fpl* wicker goods
verificar to check
vermelho(a) red
verniz *m* varnish
vertigem *f* dizziness ; vertigo
vespa *f* wasp
véspera *f* the day before ; the eve
vestiário *m* cloakroom ; changing room
vestido *m* dress
vestir to dress ; to wear
  vestir-se to get dressed
vestuário *m* clothes
veterinário(a) *m/f* vet
vez *f* time
  às vezes occasionally ; sometimes
  uma vez once
  duas vezes twice
  muitas vezes often
via *f* lane
via via
  via aérea by air mail
  via nasal to be inhaled
  via oral orally

viaduto *m* viaduct ; flyover
viagem *f* trip ; journey
  viagem de negócios business trip
viajante *m/f* traveller
viajar to travel
vida *f* life
vidros *mpl* glassware
vila *f* small town
vinagre *m* vinegar
vindima *f* harvest *(of grapes)*
vinho *m* wine
vir to come
virar to turn
  vire à direita turn right
  vire à esquerda turn left
vírgula *f* comma
visitar to visit
vista *f* view
  com linda vista with a beautiful view
visto *m* visa
vitela *f* veal
viúvo(a) *m/f* widower/widow
vivenda *f* chalet ; villa
viver to live
vivo(a) alive
vizinho(a) *m/f* neighbour
você(s) you
volante *m* steering wheel
volta *f* turn
  à volta de about
  em volta de around
  dar uma volta to go for a short walk/ride
voltagem *f* voltage
voltar to return *(go/come back)*
  volto já I'll be back in a minute
vomitar to vomit
voo *m* flight
  voo fretado charter flight

  voo normal scheduled flight
vos you ; to you
vós you
vosso yours
voz *f* voice
vulcão *m* volcano

W

WC toilet
wind-surf *m* windsurfing

X

xadrez *m* chess
xarope *m* syrup
  xarope para a tosse cough syrup
xerez *m* sherry

Z

zero zero ; nought
zona *f* zone
  zona azul permitted parking zone
  zona de banhos swimming area
  zona interdita no thoroughfare

NOUNS

Portuguese nouns are *masculine* or *feminine*, and their gender is shown by the words for **the** (**o/a**) and **a** (**um/uma**) used before them (the 'article'):

	masc.	*fem.*	*plural*
the	**o castelo**	**a mesa**	**os castelos, as mesas**
a, an	**um castelo**	**uma mesa**	**uns castelos, umas mesas**

It is usually possible to tell whether a noun is *masculine* or *feminine* by its ending:

    -o or **-or** are usually *masculine*
    -a , **-agem** , **-dade** and **-tude** tend to be *feminine*.

There are exceptions, however, and it's best to learn the noun and the article together.

PLURAL

Nouns ending in a vowel form the plural by adding **-s** , while those ending in a consonant usually add **-es** . The exceptions to this are words ending in an **-m** which change to **-ns** in the plural and words ending in **-l** which change to **-is** in the plural: e.g. **hotel – hotéis** .

NOTE: When used after the words **a** *to*, **de** *of*, **em** *in* and **por** *by*, the articles (and many other words) contract:

a + as = às	*ash*	to the
de + um = dum	*dooñ*	of a
em + uma = numa	*noo-muh*	to a
por + os = pelos	*pe-loosh*	by the

ADJECTIVES

Adjectives normally follow the nouns they describe in Portuguese, e.g. **uma maçã verde** a green apple.

Some exceptions which precede the noun are:
muito(a) a lot of; **pouco(a)** little, few; **tanto(a)** so much, so many; **primeiro(a)** first; **último(a)** last; **bom (boa)** good; **nenhum (nenhuma)** no, not any; **grande** great, big.

Portuguese adjectives have to reflect the gender of the noun they describe. To make an adjective feminine, **-o** endings change to **-a** , and **-or** and **-ês** change to **-ora** and **-esa** respectively. Otherwise they generally have the same form for both genders. Thus:

masc.	**o livro vermelho**	*fem.*	**a saia vermelha**
	the red book		the red skirt
	o homem falador		**a mulher faladora**
	the talkative man		the talkative woman

To make adjectives plural, follow the general rules given for nouns.

'My'; 'Your', 'His', 'Her'

These words also depend on the gender and number of the following noun and not on the sex of the 'owner'.

	with masc. / with fem.	with plural nouns
my	**o meu / a minha**	**os meus / as minhas**
his/her/its/your	**o seu / a sua**	**os seus / as suas**
our	**o nosso / a nossa**	**os nossos / as nossas**
their/your	**o seu / a sua**	**os seus / as suas**

NOTE: Since **o seu** , **a sua** , etc can mean **his**, **her**, **your**, etc, Portuguese will often replace them with the words for **of him**, **of her**, **of you**, etc (**dele** , **dela** , **de você** , etc) in order to avoid confusion:

os livros *dela*	her books
os livros *de você*	your books
os livros *deles*	their books

PRONOUNS

SUBJECT		OBJECT	
I	**eu** *eoo*	me	**me** *muh*
you (*informal*)	**tu** *too*	you (*informal*)	**te** *tuh*
you	**você** *vo-se*	you	**o/a** *oo/uh*
he	**ele** *el*	him	**o** *oo*
she	**ela** *e-luh*	her	**a** *uh*
it	**ele/ela** *el/e-luh*	it	**o/a** *oo/uh*
we	**nós** *nosh*	us	**nos** *noosh*
you (*informal*)	**vocês** *vo-sesh*	you (*informal*)	**os/as** *oosh/ush*
you	**vós** *vosh*	you	**vos** *voosh*
they (*masc.*)	**eles** *elsh*	them (*masc.*)	**os** *oosh*
they (*fem.*)	**elas** *e-lush*	them (*fem.*)	**as** *ush*

189

NOTES

1. **YOU** The polite form of addressing someone would be with **o Senhor** or **a Senhora** using the **(s)he** form or the verb and the object pronoun **o/a**. The semi-formal **you** is **você** and the informal **you** is **tu** (like French and Spanish).

2. Subject pronouns are normally not used except for emphasis or to avoid confusion:

    eu **vou para Lisboa e** *ele* **vai para Coimbra**
    I'm going to Lisbon and he's going to Coimbra

3. Object pronouns are usually placed after the verb and joined with a hyphen:

    vejo-*o*   I see him

However, in sentences beginning with a 'question word' or a 'negative word' the pronoun goes in front of the verb:

    quando *o* viu?   when did you see him?
    não *o* vi   I did not see him

Also, in sentences beginning with **that** and **who**, etc ('subordinate clauses') the pronoun precedes the verb:

    sei que *o* viu   I know that you saw him
    o homem que *o* viu   the man who saw him

4. **Me** also = **to me** and **nos** = **to us**, but **lhe** = **to him/to her/to it/to you** *(formal)*, **te** = **to you** *(informal)* and **lhes** = **to them/to you**.

5. When two pronouns are used together they are often shortened. The verb will also change spelling if it ends in **-r** , **-s** , **-z** or a nasal sound:

    dá-mo   **(= dá + me + o)**   he gives me it
    dê-lho   **(= dê + lhe + o)**   give him it
    fá-lo   **(= faz + o)**   he does it
    dão-nos (= dão + os or **dão + nos)**   they give them
                                    or they give us

6. The pronoun following a preposition has the same form as the subject pronoun, except for **mim** (me), **si** (you – *formal*), **ti** (you – *informal*).

VERBS

There are three main patterns of endings for verbs in Portuguese – those ending **-ar**, **-er** and **-ir** in the dictionary.

CANT**AR**	TO SING		COM**ER**	TO EAT
canto	I sing		**como**	I eat
cantas	you sing		**comes**	you eat
canta	(s)he/it sings/you sing		**come**	(s)he/it eats/you eat
cantamos	we sing		**comemos**	we eat
cantais	you sing		**comeis**	you eat
cantam	they/you sing		**comem**	they/you eat

PART**IR**	TO LEAVE
parto	I leave
partes	you leave
parte	(s)he/it leaves/you leave
partimos	we leave
partis	you leave
partem	they/you leave

And in the past tense:

cantei	I sang		**comi**	I ate
cantaste	you sang		**comeste**	you ate
cantou	(s)he/it/you sang		**comeu**	(s)he/it/you ate
cantámos	we sang		**comemos**	we ate
cantastes	you sang		**comestes**	you ate
cantaram	they/you sang		**comeram**	they/you ate

parti	I left
partiste	you left
partiu	(s)he/it/you left
partimos	we left
partistes	you left
partiram	they/you left

THE VERB 'TO BE'

There are two different Portuguese verbs for to be - **ser** and **estar**.

Ser is used to describe a permanent place or state:

sou inglês	I am English
é uma praia	it's a beach

Estar is used to describe a temporary state or where something is located temporarily:

como está?	how are you?
estou constipado	I've got a cold
onde está o carro?	where's the car?

SER	TO BE	ESTAR	TO BE
sou	I am	**estou**	I am
és	you are	**estás**	you are
é	(s)he/it is/you are	**está**	(s)he/it is/you are
somos	we are	**estamos**	we are
sois	you are	**estais**	you are
são	they/you are	**estão**	they/you are

Other common irregular verbs include:

TER	TO HAVE	IR	TO GO
tenho	I have	**vou**	I go
tens	you have	**vais**	you go
tem	(s)he/it has/you have	**vai**	(s)he/it goes/you go
temos	we have	**vamos**	we go
tendes	you have	**ides**	you go
têm	they/you have	**vão**	they/you go

POSSO	TO BE ABLE	VER	TO SEE
posso	I can	**vejo**	I see
podes	you can	**vês**	you see
pode	(s)he/it has/you can	**vê**	(s)he/it goes/you sees
podemos	we can	**vemos**	we see
podeis	you can	**vedes**	you see
têm	they/you can	**vêem**	they/you see